What Readers Are Saying About
ExpressionEngine 2: A Quick-Start Guide

Ryan helps make the entire process of working with ExpressionEngine
extremely clear. *ExpressionEngine 2: A Quick-Start Guide* is a great
start for newbies but also a great reference for us pros, with some
oft-neglected features and techniques.

► **Lea Alcantara**
    Creative Principal/Chief Hired Gun, Lealea Design

ExpressionEngine 2: A Quick-Start Guide is a must-have asset for all
developers new to ExpressionEngine. How I wish this book had been
written when I first started using ExpressionEngine.

► **Sean Smith**
    Head Developer, Create Sean Web Design

Since the goal of the book is to finish a complete website, it's hard to
put the book down until the end. Ryan's writing style turns what ini-
tially seems like a daunting challenge into a fun, easy, and rewarding
learning experience.

► **Joey Pfeifer**
    Designer

An excellent introduction to ExpressionEngine 2.

► **Greg Salt**
    Purple Dogfish

ExpressionEngine 2

A Quick-Start Guide

ExpressionEngine 2
A Quick-Start Guide

Ryan Irelan

The Pragmatic Bookshelf
Raleigh, North Carolina   Dallas, Texas

Our Pragmatic courses, workshops, and other products can help you and your team create better software and have more fun. For more information, as well as the latest Pragmatic titles, please visit us at

http://www.pragprog.com

Printed in the United States of America.

ISBN-10: 1-934356-52-2
ISBN-13: 978-1-934356-52-4
Printed on acid-free paper.
P2.0 printing, June 2010
Version: 2010-5-18

Contents

Acknowledgments

This book wasn't created by just one person. I'm thankful to have had so many different people help me out both directly and indirectly.

To Mike Clark, who connected me with the wonderful people at The Pragmatic Programmers, for his continued support.

To Susannah Davidson Pfalzer for her work as my editor and motivator.

To Greg Storey for his mentorship, friendship, and support. I hold him personally responsible for any success I may have.

To the fine folks at EllisLab: Rick Ellis, Leslie Camacho, Derek Jones, Derek Allard, Lisa Wess, Robin Sowell, and their entire support staff.

To Lea Alcantara, Greg Salt, Sean Smith, Kaan Karaca, Dan Wohlbruck, Drew Warkentin, and Joey Pfeifer for their valuable feedback.

To my friends and colleagues for their support: Ethan Marcotte, Stephen Caver, Helenita Johnston, Matt Clark, Dan Benjamin, Dan Cederholm, Jeffrey Zeldman, Mark Huot, Brian Warren, Jenn Lukas, Jason Santa Maria, Manton Reece, James Duncan Davidson, Damon Clinkscales, Phi Sanders, Jason Moore, David Tull, Brian Carter, Doug Payne, Greg Cangialosi, Jamie Pittock, Simon Collison, Robert Eerhart, Ryan Masuga, Luke Dorny, Nevin Lyne, Ryan Sims, Noah Stokes, Brandon Kelly, Leevi Graham, Kenny Meyers, Erik Reagan, Mitchell Kimbrough, Paul Burdick, Veerle Pieters, Gert Leyseele, and all of the readers and contributors to EE Insider.

To Mom and Dad for their encouragement and support.

And, finally, to my wife Alexandra for supporting my endeavors and for her love and partnership.

Foreword

It's been nearly ten years since I wrote my first web publishing application, a blog tool called pMachine, which would become the predecessor to ExpressionEngine. Ten years ago there were only some 3 million websites in total, few of which served content dynamically. Although blogging had just been invented and there were a few software venders offering expensive content management systems (CMSs), the Web was a patchwork of mostly static brochure sites. This was about to change. Rapidly.

Today, more than 25 percent of the world is online, and the number of sites serving dynamic content well exceeds 100 million. Blogs have gone totally mainstream, and CMSs are ubiquitous and cheap. A revolution in personal and corporate communication happened in the blink of an eye. For those of us who have been in the field since the beginning, it's been a very exciting and satisfying ride. For those interested in web publishing, the opportunities and choices have never been greater or more powerful.

Henry Mencken, long before the Web was invented, quipped, "Freedom of press is limited to those who own one." He had no idea that soon anyone with little more than an Internet connection and a web browser could "own" such a press. The book you hold teaches how you too can join this revolution and reach a potential audience of well over 1 billion people.

As I write this, ExpressionEngine just turned 2, and I can think of no one more qualified to teach it than Ryan Irelan. When people ask me what the best feature of ExpressionEngine is, I usually say "our community," and Ryan is a shining example of just such a "feature." Ryan has distinguished himself as an educator and advocate of Expression-Engine and as a member of our Professionals Network. He has touched thousands of people in our discussion forums, through his own ExpressionEngine online resources, and with his web clientele.

Happy publishing!

Rick Ellis (CEO of EllisLab and creator of ExpressionEngine)
March 2010

Introduction

What started out as a simple publishing tool for recording artist Nancy Sinatra has been cultivated by EllisLab and the community into a robust content management and web publishing system. Over the past six years, ExpressionEngine has seen phenomenal growth, not only in terms of features, flexibility, and extensibility but also in the size of the community of web designers, developers, and marketers who build websites with it. Whether you're building a small site or a large corporate undertaking, ExpressionEngine is becoming the tool of choice. With the release of ExpressionEngine 2, this is a great time to learn Expression-Engine and become part of this passionate and thriving community.

This book gives you the information and tools you need to begin developing websites with ExpressionEngine. You'll get up and running on ExpressionEngine quickly while learning best practices. You'll learn everything you need to build a basic ExpressionEngine-powered website, and this book lays the foundation you can build on to become an ExpressionEngine expert. We'll get hands-on immediately: throughout the book, I'll show how to build an entire website using ExpressionEngine, and you'll learn the main site-building techniques along the way.

What's New in ExpressionEngine 2

ExpressionEngine 2 is a large step forward in terms of functionality and platform. The entire application was rewritten using the CodeIgniter PHP framework, making add-on development easier. ExpressionEngine 2 has about fifty new features that help make building websites on ExpressionEngine better than before. Here are a few of the most notable new features:

- Redesigned and more customizable Control Panel interface

- File Manager for easy upload and retrieval of site images and files

- Accessories add-ons that allow you to strategically display content or data in specific parts of the Control Panel

- More easily customizable member theme templates

Chapter 8, *Managing Files and Images*, on page 123 is dedicated to the new File Manager and explores its features and functionality. In the final chapter, Chapter 11, *Extending ExpressionEngine with Add-Ons*, on page 169, you'll learn about all of the different add-on types, including the new accessories.

Those are just the highlights. This book covers everything you need to get started with ExpressionEngine 2. ExpressionEngine continues to evolve. See the *Online Resources* section for ways to keep up to date with the latest ExpressionEngine changes and versions.

Who Should Read This Book

This book is written for web designers, web developers, and managers of web or interactive teams. To get the most from this book, you should have experience building websites and using content management systems.

To successfully follow along in this book, you should know how to use HTML, how to use CSS (you'll be able to download sample code templates for the example site we'll build), and how to upload files to a web server and set permissions. If you've installed and configured other content management systems or blogging applications, then you should have no problem getting started with this book.

What's in This Book?

This book is broken up into three parts:

- *Getting Started with ExpressionEngine*: You'll first learn how to install the software and then learn how to make content appear in templates. This part is the appetizer and will teach you the basics of ExpressionEngine upon which you'll build throughout the book.

- *Building Your First ExpressionEngine Site*: This is the main course. Here you'll build, step-by-step, a basic newspaper website in ExpressionEngine. By the time you're finished with this part, you'll have learned all of the necessary skills and techniques needed to successfully build websites in ExpressionEngine.

- *Digging In*: The third and final part is the icing on the cake. You'll learn some advanced site-building techniques and use one of the biggest new features in ExpressionEngine 2: the File Manager. You'll also learn some advanced techniques you can use to make your ExpressionEngine templates smarter and more flexible. You'll also learn how to optimize your ExpressionEngine website for maximum performance and how to extend the functionality of ExpressionEngine with add-ons (accessories, plug-ins, modules, and extensions).

How to Read This Book

Depending on your level of experience, the approach you take with the book may differ. Here are some ways to get the most of the material.

If you're new to ExpressionEngine and have never used it before, start with Chapter 1, *Installing ExpressionEngine*, on page 3. You can then comfortably proceed to Chapter 2, *Hands-on Templating*, on page 19 to prepare for the rest of the book. I encourage you to progress through the book in order so you get the most from the information provided.

If you have some prior experience with ExpressionEngine, you can skip the first two chapters and jump right into building an ExpressionEngine website. This process begins in Chapter 3, *What We're Building*, on page 37 and continues throughout the rest of the book. Even if you have built a website with ExpressionEngine before, the techniques and best practices covered may be new or beneficial to you. I encourage you to follow along through the entire site-building process.

For the best experience, the second part of the book should be read straight through from beginning to end. However, you can read the third part in any order that makes the most sense to you.

All of the code, images, and other files needed to build the website in Part II are provided in the downloadable code files. You can find information on how to download the site templates in the following section.

Online Resources

This book has its own web page, http://pragprog.com/titles/riexen, where you can find more information about the book and interact in the following ways:

- You can download all of the static and fully coded templates for the sample site.
- You can participate in a discussion forum with other readers, ExpressionEngine enthusiasts, and me.
- You can help improve the book by reporting errata, including content suggestions and typos.

Also, if you own the ebook, you can click the gray boxes before each code listing to download the code excerpts while building the sample site.

The ExpressionEngine software is just one part of the picture. It's the community of passionate users and helpful developers who make it a reliable platform on which to build a website. Here are some community resources to explore:

- *ExpressionEngine Forums*: http://expressionengine.com/forums
- *EE Insider*: http://eeinsider.com
- *Devot:ee*: http://devot-ee.com
- *ExpressionEngine Wiki*: http://expressionengine.com/wiki

My goal with this book is to teach you the basics and inspire you to explore, learn, and build powerful, flexible, and *amazing* websites with ExpressionEngine. Whether you're new to ExpressionEngine or have some experience, we'll take the journey together, and I'll guide you each step of the way.

Ryan Irelan
March 2010

Part I

Getting Started with ExpressionEngine

Chapter 1

Installing ExpressionEngine

Our first order of business is to get ExpressionEngine installed and running. After that we'll create a template, tour the Control Panel, and learn about development environments.

First you need to follow a few steps to prepare to install ExpressionEngine on your server.

1.1 Evaluating Hosting

Once you download the Server Wizard, unzip it and use your FTP client to upload the ee_wizard directory to the web root of your server. In your browser, go to the wizard [1], and you should see a page similar to Figure 1.1, on the next page.

Step 1 checks your database server. You should have your database server information at hand for this test. The database check attempts to connect to your database using the login information you provided and checks that MySQL is configured so ExpressionEngine can function properly.

Fill out the form, entering your MySQL server address, your MySQL username and password, and the MySQL database name. If for some reason the wizard cannot connect to your database server, it will report an error message at the bottom of the next page.

---

1. http://yourdomain.com/ee_wizard

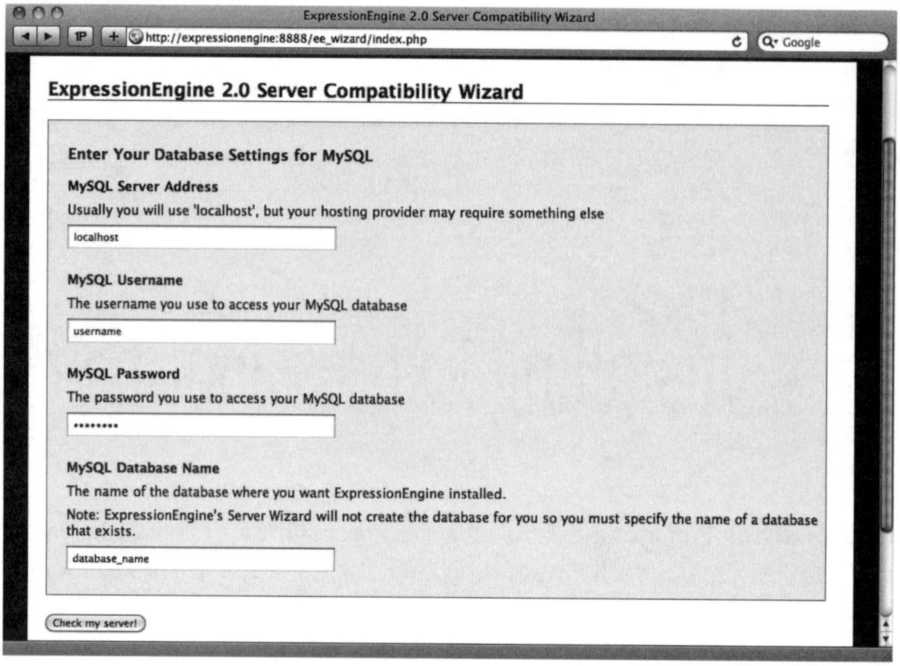

Figure 1.1: CHECKING THE DATABASE CONNECTION WITH THE EXPRESSIONENGINE SERVER WIZARD.

If you receive an error, double-check your login information, database name, and server location. If you continue to have issues, contact your web host support or your server administrator. In my experience, most issues with connecting to the database are related to login information and the server location information.

If the wizard is able to successfully connect to your database server and database, you should be forwarded to the next page of the wizard.

Step 2 checks your server for all the requirements and suggested libraries. Those marked with a red "No" are not supported on your server or hosting account, while those marked with a green "Yes" are supported. If you have a red "No" next to a required item, you should contact your web host support or server administrator and ask about it. Going forward with the ExpressionEngine installation in spite of the missing requirements will cause the software to not function properly and will create problems.

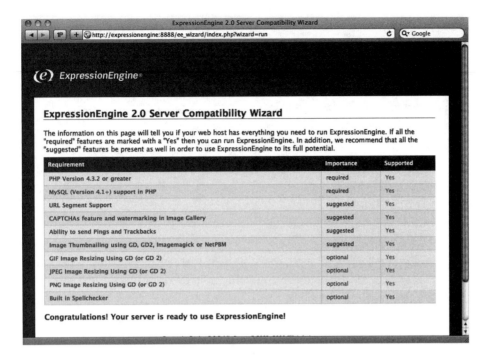

Figure 1.2: CHECKING FOR REQUIREMENTS WITH THE EXPRESSION-
ENGINE SERVER WIZARD.

If the wizard shows that all requirements have been met (including the
database test from earlier), you should see a congratulatory message at
the bottom of the page.

With your server ready to run ExpressionEngine, let's move forward
and download the software.

1.2 Getting the Software

ExpressionEngine is not open source software and cannot be freely distributed across the Internet.

ExpressionEngine is a commercial product, and there are licensing fees
involved. The only way to get the software is from the ExpressionEngine
website.[2]

---

2. http://expressionengine.com

> ### Can I Use the Trial Version?
>
> You can download a limited, 30-day trial of ExpressionEngine. Because the source code is encrypted, it requires some special software, the Zend Optimizer, to run. Additionally, you are not able to change the name of the system directory.
>
> To get the most from this book, you should use a full version of ExpressionEngine.

Here are the available licenses:

- *Freelancer*: $99.95 and restricted to web professionals who want to use ExpressionEngine to build their own company website.
- *Noncommercial*: $149.95 and can be used only on nonprofit and personal websites.
- *Commercial*: $299.95 and has no restrictions in how it is used. This version is for commercial sites run by for-profit or commercial companies.

To get a full list of the features available for each type of license, I encourage you to visit the ExpressionEngine website for a side-by-side comparison of the licensing options.[3]

Once you choose the license that is right for your situation, purchase and then download the software from the ExpressionEngine site so you can install it.

1.3 Installing ExpressionEngine

Once the download is complete, you should have a .zip file. Unzip this file on your desktop.

Uploading the Files

You are now ready to move the files from the local computer and onto the server. To upload the ExpressionEngine software to your server, follow these steps:

1. Connect to your server using your FTP client software.

---

3. http://expressionengine.com/overview/pricing/

2. Upload all text files in ASCII mode and all images in binary mode.

3. Once the upload is complete, find the system directory that you just uploaded on your server. The creators of ExpressionEngine recommend that you rename this directory to something that is more obscure. For this example, we're going to name our system directory ringo. After making the change, open the index.php file, and update the $system_path variable to reflect the new directory name. It should now look like this:

$system_path = './ringo';

Setting Permissions

One final step before running the Installation Wizard is to make sure all the file permissions are correct. Incorrect file permissions can cause headaches when installing and using ExpressionEngine.

The following files must be set to permissions 666 (Unix or Mac OS X) or Writeable on Windows:

- ringo/expressionengine/config/config.php
- ringo/expressionengine/config/database.php

You must set the following files to permissions of 777 (Unix or Mac OS X) or Writeable on Windows:

- images/avatars/uploads
- images/captchas
- images/member_photos
- images/pm_attachments
- images/signature_attachments
- images/uploads
- ringo/expressionengine/cache

Running the Installation Wizard

The Installation Wizard checks that all the ExpressionEngine files are present and then populates the database with data needed to run ExpressionEngine. It's a simple, painless process but does require that the database connection information is close by. Let's get started.

In your web browser, go to the domain where you have uploaded the ExpressionEngine files, and add your system directory to the end of the domain so it looks like this: http://yoursite.com/system (we changed the system directory to ringo). This will bring you to the Installation Wizard.

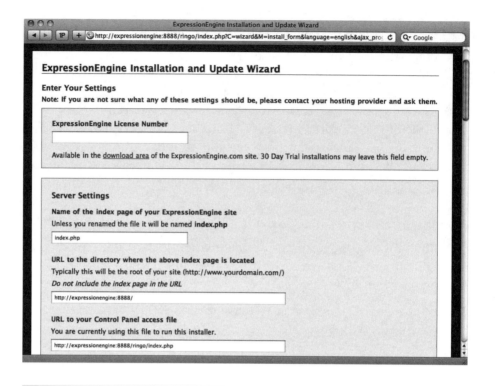

Figure 1.3: FILLING OUT THE SERVER SETTINGS DURING INSTALLATION

Click the button to begin, and then choose a new install by clicking the text "Click here to install a brand new copy of ExpressionEngine." Agree to the software license, and then click Submit.

The next step is to input your server settings and database connection details and create an administrator account. You should see a screen that looks similar to Figure 1.3.

Follow the instructions that are listed with each area on the settings page of the wizard. You can also check or uncheck ExpressionEngine modules that you would like to have installed. These modules can be installed at any time, so it's safe to leave the default settings.

For the "Choose your default template design" option, select Agile Records. Although you won't need this for the site we'll build later in the book, the sample site will help you become familiar with ExpressionEngine.

Once completed, click Install ExpressionEngine! If the installation was successful, you should see the success screen.

You should now delete the installer directory from your server. It's located in the expressionengine directory in your system directory. This is an important security precaution. If you leave the directory on your server, someone could potentially run the Installation Wizard in their browser and reinstall the software, wiping out your database and your website. ExpressionEngine has a safeguard against this by "locking" your installation, but it's still a good idea to remove the directory to eliminate the chance of unauthorized access to your site.

1.4   Exploring the ExpressionEngine Directories and Files

If you're not already connected, open your FTP client software, and connect to your server where you installed ExpressionEngine. Navigate to the web root where the ExpressionEngine files are located. Let's take a quick look at the directories and files that will be most important while learning to use ExpressionEngine:

images/
> Stored in this directory are the images that ExpressionEngine will use in your site. These images are for member avatars, photos, smileys, and user uploads via the Control Panel.

index.php
> This is the main file that processes all requests to the Expression-Engine site. As we progress in the book, you'll notice that this file appears in the URL of your site. Leave this file as is, and don't edit it any further.

expressionengine/installer/
> Ha, tricked you! This directory shouldn't be on your server if you were following directions. If you still have this file on your server, please delete it now.

system/ (renamed by me to ringo)
> This directory contains all the files that make ExpressionEngine run. It's also the directory you'll use in the web browser to access the site's Control Panel.

system/expressionengine/third_party
> This directory is where you will put any third-party add-ons you want to use with ExpressionEngine. This is different from previous

versions of ExpressionEngine where the add-ons went in separate directories. The four types of add-ons that go in this directory are accessories, extensions, plug-ins, and modules.

Accessories are new to ExpressionEngine and allow you to display content in tabs at the bottom of the Control Panel.

Extensions are chunks of code (in a file that begins with ext) that typically modify how the Control Panel works. You can download first- and third-party extensions from the ExpressionEngine website.[4]

By offering additional functionality, plug-ins allow you to control and alter the type of information that is displayed in the site templates. You can review a list of available plug-ins on the ExpressionEngine website.[5]

Modules are applications that can be plugged into the ExpressionEngine system to add some major functionality. Modules usually have their own administration pages in the Control Panel. You can browse the available modules on the ExpressionEngine website.[6]

system/expressionengine/config

The config directory contains files with configuration data that is specific to your installation of ExpressionEngine. This includes database connection information in the database.php file and includes the site URL and Control Panel URL in the config.php file. The ExpressionEngine Installation Wizard set up these files for us, so for now you can leave these files alone.

themes/

This directory contains themes that control the look of different parts of ExpressionEngine, including the Control Panel.

You'll notice that we skipped over a lot of the files and directories. Many of them are not relevant to what we're doing right now, but some will come up over the course of the book and as we become more experienced with ExpressionEngine. The next step in learning about ExpressionEngine is to experience the Control Panel, where we'll be spending a lot of time configuring and managing our website.

---

4. http://expressionengine.com/downloads/addons/category/extensions/
5. http://expressionengine.com/downloads/addons/category/plugins/
6. http://expressionengine.com/downloads/addons/category/modules/

1.5 Touring the Control Panel

The ExpressionEngine Control Panel is the nerve center for your site. Here you manage and publish content, create and edit templates, and configure any of the many settings and preferences for your Expression-Engine-powered website.

To gain access to the Control Panel, you have to enter the username and password you created during installation. In your web browser, navigate to your system directory.[7] Once there you should see a login screen. Log in, and you're brought to the Control Panel home page.

We're going to tour just a few of the main features of the Control Panel; you'll find out about many more features later as we build the sample site in the second part of the book.

Control Panel Home

The Control Panel home page (see Figure 1.4, on the next page) provides you with easy access to the three main ways to manage your ExpressionEngine site: create, modify, and view. From the home page, you can easily create or modify content, manage comments, access the ExpressionEngine User Guide, or manage your website templates.

You can also search the Control Panel (for example, searching for *template* will return all the areas in the Control Panel where you can manage a template) or access the Quick Links to easily access bookmarked Control Panel pages.

Publishing Content

Click the Content button and then Publish at the top left of the Control Panel to add new content to the site. ExpressionEngine prompts you to choose which *channel* you'd like to use[8]. A channel is a bucket for your content. As we build the website in the second part of this book, we'll be creating multiple channels for our content.

Select News from the two channels listed. This is the screen where you add content to your site.

---

7. Such as http://mysite.com/system. Yours should have a customized name (I used ringo, remember?).

8. If you didn't choose the Agile Records site during installation, then no channels will appear.

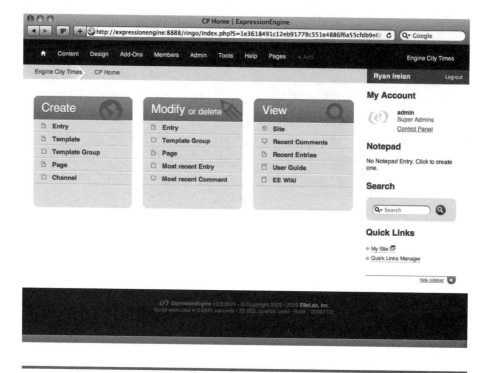

Figure 1.4: EXPLORING THE CONTROL PANEL HOME PAGE

Editing Content

The Edit screen (see Figure 1.5, on the facing page) provides an overview of all content on your site, whether it's in draft form or published. When you click the Content button and then Edit, you see several channel entries listed. As we build out our ExpressionEngine site, this will be an even longer list of channel entries.

Also notice the search functionality at the top of the page. It will let you search and sort content by channel, category, status (Open or Closed), and date range. Additionally, you can limit the search to just specific pieces of content, such as titles or comments. Once your site is populated with hundreds of content items, it becomes an indispensable tool for managing your content in ExpressionEngine.

The list of content is comprised of several columns, each providing an overview of the content pieces. Click the title of the sample content, and you will see the Edit page for that item. Here you can edit the content and save your changes.

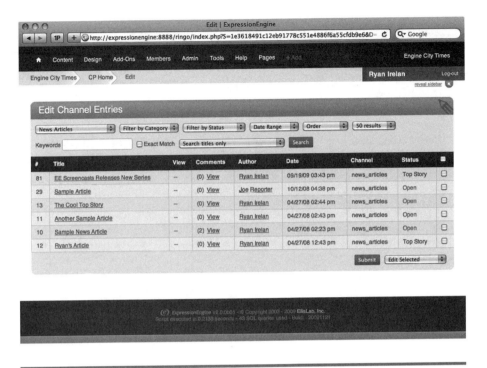

Figure 1.5: VIEWING THE EDIT SCREEN IN THE CONTROL PANEL

From the main Edit page, you also have the ability to delete content—either individually or in bulk. You do this by checking the box (on the far right) next to each item and then using the drop-down menu at the bottom to select which action you'd like to take. Deleting content cannot be undone, so be careful!

Managing Templates

The Template Manager (see Figure 1.6, on the next page) is where you manage all the templates (HTML markup and ExpressionEngine tags) that make your site come to life in the web browser. To access the Template Manager, click the Design button at the top of the Control Panel and then click Template Manager under the Templates menu item.

Templates are organized by groups, which are listed on the far left of the Template Manager page. You should see four groups: about, global_embeds, * news, and search. The asterisk next to the third group denotes that its index template is the home page of the site.

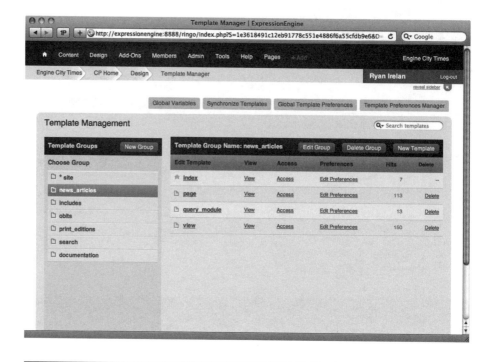

Figure 1.6: MANAGING YOUR EXPRESSIONENGINE TEMPLATES

The middle of the page is where you can access each individual template of the selected group. Clicking the name will let you edit the template. Additionally, at the top of the list of templates there are three buttons that allow you to edit the selected template groups, as well as add a new template or delete a group.

Administering the Site

Let's continue our tour of the Control Panel by exploring the site administration options.

The Admin area is where you configure and tweak your Expression-Engine installation and consists of several sections to give you control over how your site is set up. To access the Admin area, click the Admin button at the top of the Control Panel, and then choose Overview (at the bottom of the list).

Channel Administration

The Channel Administration section is at the top of page when you access the Admin area of the Control Panel. Please explore each area of Channel Administration on your own, but here are some of the areas that will be most important to you as you begin building your first website with ExpressionEngine:

- *Channels*: Here you create, delete, and edit the content channels on your ExpressionEngine website. This is where you can define the different types of the content that will appear on the site.

- *Categories*: In this subsection of Channel Administration, you can add new category groups and categories, as well as manage all of your existing categories. The default site we installed comes with two category groups.

- *Custom fields*: ExpressionEngine allows you to create custom fields that fit the type of content in your website. Here you can manage those custom fields and custom field groups.

System Administration

Further down the page, System Administration gives you access to some of the finer controls of the ExpressionEngine software. Although most of the settings here won't be necessary to get started with ExpressionEngine (the defaults will work just fine), I do want to point out a couple of areas that you should be familiar with:

- *Config Editor*: In this area you can alter settings in your config.php file.

- *Output and Debugging*: Although you may not use this immediately, it is good to know where the debugging settings are located. These settings allow you to enable special debugging output when you need some extra information to help solve a problem while building your ExpressionEngine-powered website.

Tools for Managing Your ExpressionEngine Site

The Tools section of the Control Panel offers you some additional options to manage your ExpressionEngine site. Of these tools, the most useful to you will most likely be the Data tools. Access the Tools area by clicking the Tools button at the top of the page, and select Data.

Consisting of four different tools for advanced management of your data, the one tool you'll use most often is Clear Cached Data so you can make sure the site is always serving up the latest content. The SQL Manager tool allows you view and query the ExpressionEngine database tables and may be useful when you're more experienced with ExpressionEngine.

Explore the other tools in the section. The various logs available will help make troubleshooting easier, and you can use the Communicate section to send email to members.

Managing Your User Account

The My Account area gives you access to manage all of your personal account details, including email address, profile, username and password, and Control Panel customizations. To access this area, click Control Panel (under the My Account heading) in the sidebar of the Control Panel. If the sidebar is hidden, click "reveal sidebar" near the top right of the Control Panel to make it appear.

Quick Links

At the right-bottom side of the Control Panel is a small menu that is very useful while working within ExpressionEngine (see Figure 1.7, on the facing page). By default there is just one item in the list: Quick Links Manager.

Use the Quick Links Manager to customize the links that appear in the Quick Links list. Some useful examples are a link to a dictionary website for easy reference, links to related sites, and links to site-specific documentation.

A dictionary quick link will be useful as we're adding content to our site, so let's create a link that will lead us to Dictionary.com. Click Quick Links Manager in the list.

Give the link the title of "Dictionary" and a URL of http://dictionary.com. Click Submit, and the new dictionary link appears in the Quick Links menu. Be sure to click the Dictionary link to test it!

1.6 What We Learned

In this chapter we installed ExpressionEngine and took a brief tour of the Control Panel. What we've learned will prepare us for the next chapter where we dig in and learn how to create and view templates.

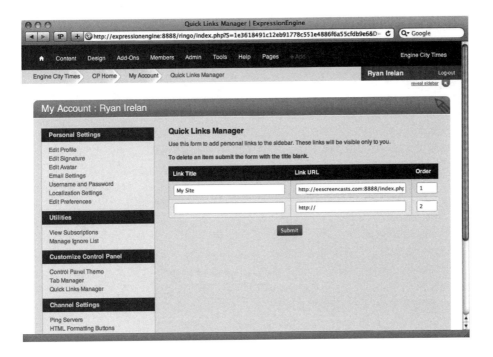

Figure 1.7: ADDING QUICK LINKS TO THE CONTROL PANEL

Before going on, however, take a few minutes to poke around the Control Panel and become even more familiar with how it works. Although I'll cover specific functionality throughout the book, it will make the learning process easier if you become as familiar as possible with Control Panel interface in this early stage.

Chapter 2

Hands-on Templating

Now that we've successfully installed and configured ExpressionEngine, let's jump right in and create our first web page. As we progress, we'll learn not only about templates but about ExpressionEngine variables and tags. By the end of the chapter, we'll have created a simple web page that displays our contact information and includes some blog entries. The work in this chapter will prepare us for the task of building our first website with ExpressionEngine.

2.1 Building Our First Template

Let's head back to the Control Panel (log in again, if necessary) so we can build our first template.

As you noticed in the previous chapter when we explored the Control Panel, ExpressionEngine has automatically created a series of template groups and templates during installation. But let's not worry about them right now. It's quicker and easier, and—most importantly—we will learn more if we just start from scratch. So, we will create our own template group and template for our new web page.

To create a new template group, click Template Group in the Create box on the home page of the Control Panel. We are now presented with the form for creating a new template group. Template group names must be a single word or multiple words connected by either underscores or hyphens. Spaces between words are not allowed (for example my_template is valid, while my template is not).

Since we're creating a single page with our contact information to which we can point business associates and friends, name the template group

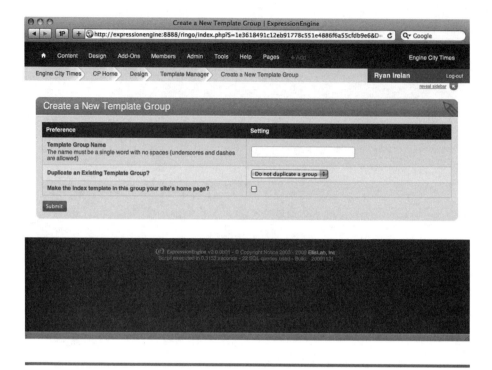

Figure 2.1: CREATING A NEW TEMPLATE GROUP

"contact." Some other options are available when creating a new template group (see Figure 2.1), but we can leave them as is for now.

Click Submit to create the new template group. ExpressionEngine pops you back to the Template Management view. To get into the template group, select it from the list on the far left. You'll notice that there is already a template there called index with a small icon of a house next to it. What is this template? Well, ExpressionEngine creates an index template automatically when we create a new template group.

For right now, we'll ignore the index template and create our own. At the top right of the template list, click the red New Template button. Let's call this new template my_info. We want the template type to be "web page," and we want ExpressionEngine to create an empty template.[1] Click Create to create the template.

---

1. You do have the option of creating a new template by cloning an existing template, but in this instance we want to create an empty template.

The Different Types of Templates

In ExpressionEngine you can create six types of templates:

- *Web Page*: Use this type to create templates to display in the web browser. This is the template type that you will use most often.
- *RSS Page*: If you need to create an RSS feed for your site, you should use this template type.
- *CSS*: If you are using ExpressionEngine to store your CSS, you will want to select this template type. ExpressionEngine tags are not parsed in CSS templates.
- *JavaScript*: This template type should be used for storing and outputting JavaScript in ExpressionEngine.
- *Static*: This is a simple template that is not parsed by ExpressionEngine.
- *XML*: Use this type if you want to create and serve an XML document in ExpressionEngine.

Adding Our Contact Information

After creating the template, ExpressionEngine returns us to the Template Management page. In the list of templates to the right, find my_info, and click the name. You'll notice the document icon to the left of the template name; this indicates that this is a web page template.

At the template edit page, you should now see a blank template. Click into the large edit area, and let's do something simple to start. Type your name and then save the template by clicking Update. To view it in a web browser, click the red View Rendered Template button (at the top right). You should see something like the screenshot in Figure 2.2, on the following page.

Adding HTML to Our Template

Of course, ExpressionEngine templates can do more than just display simple, plain text. You can put in any valid HTML markup you want, and it will render properly in the browser. Let's go ahead and give our plain my_info template a little something extra.

But before we add any HTML to our template, let's first put in the proper document header and DOCTYPE. Put the following code in the my_info template, replacing the text we had in there. Notice that your name now lives between the body tags.

Figure 2.2: RENDERING YOUR NAME IN THE BROWSER

BasicsofTemplating/header.html

```
<!DOCTYPE HTML PUBLIC "-//W3C//DTD HTML 4.01 Transitional//EN"
        "http://www.w3.org/TR/html4/loose.dtd">
<html>
 <head>
  <title>Contact Information for Ryan Irelan</title>
 </head>
 <body>
  Ryan Irelan
 </body>
</html>
```

Now we can begin adding very simple markup to our template. Let's wrap our name in an h1 tag. We'll also create an h2 tag and place the text "Contact Information" inside it. We also don't want to forget that we need to add our contact information. Something like this:

BasicsofTemplating/hello_world_simple.html

```
<h1>Ryan Irelan</h1>
<h2>Contact Information</h2>
<p>Please use this information to get in touch with me.</p>
<address>
 123 Expression Street<br />
 Engine City, USA<br />
 01234<br />
 <a href="mailto:yourname@email.com">
 youremail@email.com</a><br />
 111-555-1212
</address>
```

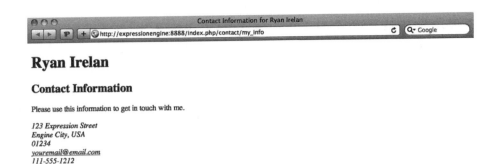

Figure 2.3: VIEWING OUR CONTACT INFORMATION

This should all sit between the body tags in the template. After you've added the previous code, save the template, and view it in your browser. You should see something like that in Figure 2.3.

The complete markup should now look like this:

BasicsofTemplating/hello_world_simple_complete.html

```
<!DOCTYPE HTML PUBLIC "-//W3C//DTD HTML 4.01 Transitional//EN"
"http://www.w3.org/TR/html4/loose.dtd">
<html>
 <head>
  <title>Contact Information for Ryan Irelan</title>
 </head>
 <body>
  <h1>Ryan Irelan</h1>
  <h2>Contact Information</h2>
  <p>Please use this information to get in touch
       with me.</p>
  <address>
   123 Expression Street<br />
   Engine City, USA<br />
   01234<br />
   <a href="mailto:yourname@email.com">
   youremail@email.com</a><br />
   111-555-1212
  </address>
 </body>
</html>
```

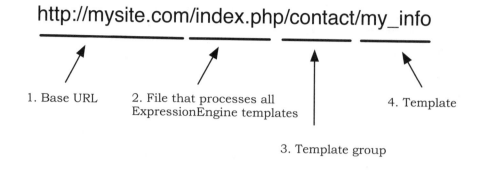

Figure 2.4: The building blocks of ExpressionEngine URLs

Congratulations, you just created your first ExpressionEngine web page! Before we go any further, a brief discussion on how Expression-Engine makes content render in the browser is in order.

2.2 Dissecting ExpressionEngine URLs

When we went to view our new web page in the browser, you might have noticed that the URL had four different parts to it (see Figure 2.4). ExpressionEngine uses the URL to determine which template (and content) to show. Let's break down the URL in Figure 2.4.

The first part of the URL is the base URL or the domain where your website is located. The second part is index.php, which is the file that processes all ExpressionEngine templates.[2]

The third part is the ExpressionEngine template group (contact) we created earlier. Lastly, the fourth part is the my_info template that we created inside the template group.

It's also possible to view the index template of a template group (remember the one that ExpressionEngine created for us?) by just appending the template group to the base URL.

For example, http://mysite.com/index.php/contact will render the same page as http://mysite.com/index.php/contact/index. If there is no template specified, ExpressionEngine will just render the index template of that

---

2. There are several ways to remove or change the index.php file from the URL. You can learn more on the ExpressionEngine website.

DISPLAYING DYNAMIC CONTENT ◀ 25

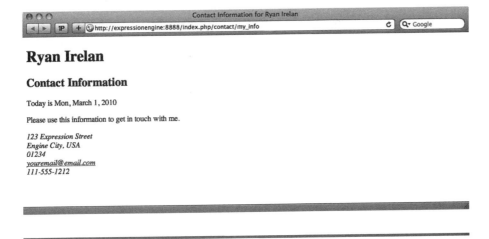

Figure 2.5: Dynamically displaying the current date and time

group. That's enough about the URLs; let's move forward and start displaying some dynamic content with our new template, shall we?

2.3 Displaying Dynamic Content

Up to this point we've displayed only static content—what we put in the template displayed exactly like that in the browser. Let's add something dynamic to our template. We want our contact information page to be timely, so using an ExpressionEngine tag,[3] let's show the current date.

Go ahead and add the following code to your template. A good place is right below the h2 tags.

BasicsofTemplating/current_date.html

```
<p>Today is {current_time format="%D, %F %d, %Y"}</p>
```

Save the template, and reload the web page in your browser. You should now see something like Figure 2.5.

The tag {current_time format="%D, %F %d, %Y"} tells ExpressionEngine to display the current date in the format we specified using the format parameter. If you've used other templating or programming languages, this syntax for displaying dates and times will look familiar to you.

---

3. We'll talk more about tags later in this chapter in Section 2.5, *Bringing Life to Templates with ExpressionEngine Tags*, on page 28.

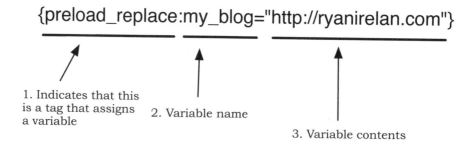

Figure 2.6: ASSIGNING A PRELOAD REPLACEMENT VARIABLE

2.4 Working with ExpressionEngine Variables

Let's continue building on our my_info template by adding some more of our own content, but this time we'll use ExpressionEngine variables to make it display. First we'll see how the variables work, and then we will learn what they do and how we can use them in our website development with ExpressionEngine.

Our First Variable

We want to be sure that the friends and business associates who visit the page also know where to go to read my weblog. Because it's important that the reader not miss this link, we want to include it twice—once at the top of the page and once at the bottom.

However, we don't want to repeat the same markup twice because down the road if we ever want to edit it and change the URL, we'll have to change the markup in two different places. This is where the variables in ExpressionEngine come in handy.

ExpressionEngine provides a way for us to assign variables right inside the template. We're going to create the variable using the preload_ replace tag. This tag has three parts (see Figure 2.6). The first part defines what type of tag it is and indicates to ExpressionEngine that this tag will create a new instance of preload replacement. The second part is the variable name, and the third part is the value we're going to assign to the variable.

`BasicsofTemplating/ee_variable_assign.php`

```
{preload_replace:my_blog="<a href='http://ryanirelan.com'>
        Visit my blog</a>"}
```

The variable name is my_blog, and the value of that variable is some HTML to create the link to my blog. Place the preload replacement tag at the very top of the my_info template. It's a good idea to keep your preload replacement tags altogether in one place. Most people prefer the top of the template; it helps keep the template more organized.

Save the template, and then reload the web page.

Oops! What happened? Where are the links to the blog? They're not there because we haven't yet placed the variable itself in the template. We only assigned the blog link to the variable but didn't tell ExpressionEngine to display it.

We add variables to the template by surrounding the variable name from the preload_replace tag with curly braces. This is what our variable will look like: {my_blog}.

Place this new variable at the top of the page, just above the h1, and then again at the bottom of the page below the last p tag. To make our link display nicely, wrap the variable in paragraph tags.

BasicsofTemplating/hello_world_with_variables.php

```
{preload_replace:my_blog="<a href="http://ryanirelan.com">
Visit my blog</a>"}

<!DOCTYPE HTML PUBLIC "-//W3C//DTD HTML 4.01 Transitional//EN"
"http://www.w3.org/TR/html4/loose.dtd">
<html>
 <head>
  <title>Contact Information for Ryan Irelan</title>
 </head>
 <body>
  <p>{my_blog}</p>
  <h1>Ryan Irelan</h1>
  <h2>Contact Information</h2>
        <p>Today is {current_time format="%D, %F %d,
        %Y"}</p>
  <p>Please use this information to get in
  touch with me.</p>
  <address>
   123 Expression Street<br />
   Engine City, USA<br />
   01234<br />
   <a href="mailto:yourname@email.com">
   youremail@email.com</a><br />
   111-555-1212
  </address>

  <p>{my_blog}</p>
 </body>
</html>
```

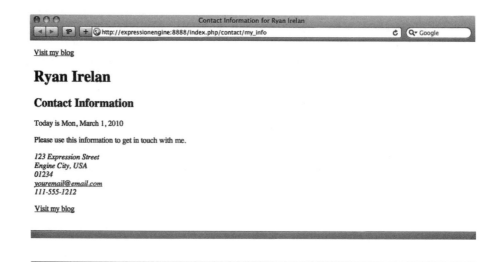

Figure 2.7: LINKING MY BLOG USING PRELOAD REPLACEMENT VARIABLES

After you make these changes, save the template. Reload the page in your browser, and you should see the links to the blog at both the top and bottom of the page, similar to Figure 2.7.

If you ever want to edit these links to my blog to point to a new URL, it's just a matter of editing in one place: at the top of the template page where we assigned the preload replacement variable. Go ahead and give it a try. Change the variable to one of your favorite websites, save the template, and reload the page.

Up to this point we've created our contact page template, dynamically displayed the date using the current_time variable, and learned how to use preload replacement variables. We're now ready to move forward and implement ExpressionEngine tags.

2.5 Bringing Life to Templates with ExpressionEngine Tags

In ExpressionEngine, the tags are what make your templates come to life. Using tags, we can dynamically pull content stored through ExpressionEngine to generate a list of categories, a comments thread, images, or blog entries. Almost anything we can input into Expression-Engine, we can also output using a tag.

How Preload Replacement Variables Work

Preload replacement variables are not much different from the variables you'll encounter in most programming languages. They are very simple to learn and a powerful way to manage content—both dynamic and static—in your template.

If you notice that your variable renders in the browser like {my_variable_name}, this probably means ExpressionEngine did not recognize it, and you have not assigned it correctly. Check your syntax and tag structure for any errors.

Finally, preload replacement variables can contain more than just static content. As you learn more about ExpressionEngine, you'll see that you can assign the variable different dynamic content depending on the page that is rendered. It's very powerful!

Building Blocks of a Tag

The first obvious sign of an ExpressionEngine tag is that it begins and ends with curly braces. All ExpressionEngine tags will follow this standard. The second thing you'll notice (Figure 2.8, on the following page) is that there are three parts to the tag, separated by colons.[4]

The first part, exp, indicates to ExpressionEngine that this is an ExpressionEngine tag. When ExpressionEngine comes across this tag in a template, it will parse it and return the data that the tag calls for.

The second part of the tag is the module name. In our example, the module is channel. ExpressionEngine is built from a collection of modules that when combined make up the powerful content management system you installed in the previous chapter.

The third part of the tag is the function inside the module preceding it. The function is some PHP code that performs a certain task and returns some type of data. In this example, the function is channel_name, which would return the name of the current channel.

---

4.   There are exceptions to this, but for now this simplified explanation will be enough.

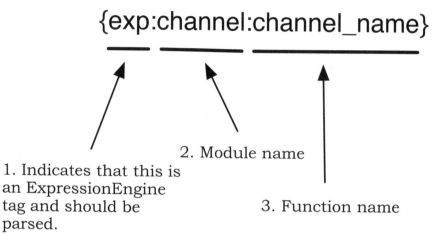

Figure 2.8: BUILDING BLOCKS OF A TAG

Tag Pairs

The tag we looked at in Figure 2.8 is a single tag. The following example is a tag pair:

`BasicsofTemplating/tag_pair_example.php`

```
{exp:channel:entries}
 Your channel entry content
{/exp:channel:entries}
```

We see the same three-part structure, but this time there is a closing tag that has a forward slash after the opening curly brace. If you neglect to close a tag pair, you'll be greeted with an error, or ExpressionEngine will just fail silently and not return anything at all.

A tag pair typically returns several different pieces of information. In this example, we are returning the entries of a channel. It tells ExpressionEngine to go fetch all the entries for the channel and then place them between the two tags.

So, how does ExpressionEngine know from which channel to pull the content? Unless we tell it exactly where to pull from, ExpressionEngine will pull content from every channel. We'll tell it using parameters.

Complete List of Tags

A lot of tags are available with the default ExpressionEngine modules. For a list of those tags, check out the official wiki: http://expressionengine.com/wiki/Complete_Tag_List.

Meet the Parameters

Parameters determine what type and how much content Expression-Engine should return. We'll use a couple of parameters to tell ExpressionEngine which channel to pull from and how many entries we'd like to show.

The parameter takes the form of parameter_name="value". This is universal across all ExpressionEngine tags, no matter whether the modules are the ones that ship with the software, those you download online from a third-party, or modules you create yourself.

```
{exp:channel:entries channel="my_weblog"}

 Channel entries here

{/exp:channel:entries}
```

Another typical parameter for the Channel Entries tag pair is the limit parameter. This, just like it says, limits the number of entries that ExpressionEngine displays in the browser. Let's limit our display to just two entries:

```
{exp:channel:entries channel="my_weblog" limit="2"}

2 channel entries here

{/exp:channel:entries}
```

That's a good start. We've told ExpressionEngine that we want to display entries from a channel, and we've indicated which channel and how many entries to show. Now we have to tell it which content to display from those entries and where.

Tag Variables

Tag variables are the single tags that live inside the tag pairs and instruct ExpressionEngine on which content should be displayed and where.

For example, a channel entry usually consists of several different parts. A basic channel entry has a title, a body, a date published, an author name, and possibly a category. Using the tag variables, we can instruct ExpressionEngine on what to display for every channel entry it returns.

Let's go back to our my_info template we created earlier and set it up to display channel entries.

We're going to use the following tag variables inside the Channel Entries tag pair:

{title} {news_body} {entry_date} {author}

It's fairly self-explanatory what each tag variable will return, so go ahead and add the following to our my_info template. Place it just above the bottom {my_blog} variable.

`BasicsofTemplating/weblog_entries.php`

```
<h3>Latest Entries from My Blog</h3>
 {exp:channel:entries channel="news" limit="2"}
 <h4>{title}</h4>
 {news_body}
 <small>Published on {entry_date format="%M %d, %Y"} by
 {author}</small>
{/exp:channel:entries}
```

I added some simple HTML to better organize the blog entry. Your complete template should now look like this (the new code is indicated by the arrows):

`BasicsofTemplating/complete_template.php`

```
{preload_replace:my_blog="<a href="http://ryanirelan.com">
Visit my blog</a>"}

<!DOCTYPE HTML PUBLIC "-//W3C//DTD HTML 4.01 Transitional//EN"
"http://www.w3.org/TR/html4/loose.dtd">
<html>
 <head>
  <title>Contact Information for Ryan Irelan</title>
 </head>
 <body>
  <p>{my_blog}</p>
```

```
   <h1>Ryan Irelan</h1>
   <h2>Contact Information</h2>
        <p>Today is {current_time format="%D, %F
        %d, %Y"}</p>
    <p>Please use this information to get in
touch with me.</p>
   <address>
    123 Expression Street<br />
    Engine City, USA<br />
    01234<br />
    <a href="mailto:yourname@email.com">
        youremail@email.com</a><br />
        111-555-1212
   </address>


►   <h3>Latest Entries from My Blog</h3>
►   {exp:channel:entries channel="news" limit="2"}
►   <h4>{title}</h4>
►   {news_body}
►   <small>Published on {entry_date
►        format="%M %d,%Y"} by {author}</small>
►   {/exp:channel:entries}
    <p>{my_blog}</p>

  </body>
</html>
```

Save the updated template, and reload the web page in your browser (see Figure 2.9, on the following page). Wow! Where did that content come from?

When we installed ExpressionEngine, we chose the Agile Record sample site, which populated ExpressionEngine with some sample channels and entries. Using the channel="news" parameter, we're pulling the latest entry from that channel. This default content is a convenient way to test our code against content without having to create any.

We now have a simple yet informative page that includes some contact information, a link to our blog, and some recent blog entries.

Using the {exp:channel:entries} tag pair, we were able to pull existing content into our page and display it using tag variables. Now that we have the basics, we're able to attack some more advanced features of creating templates in ExpressionEngine. We'll have this opportunity when we're building an entire site in the next section.

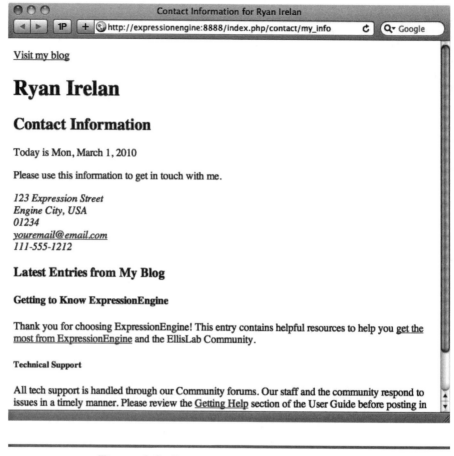

Figure 2.9: OUR COMPLETE CONTACT PAGE

2.6 What We Learned

In this chapter, we learned how to create a new template group and template and the basics of managing templates in ExpressionEngine. By creating our contact information web page, we learned how to render a simple template in the browser and display dynamic content using single tags, tag pairs, and tag variables.

While the web page we created is simple, the basic knowledge we've acquired has prepared us for the task of building an entire site in the next section of the book.

Part II

Building Our First ExpressionEngine Site

Chapter 3

What We're Building

The only way to really learn anything is to do it. Over the next few chapters we'll jump in and build our first ExpressionEngine site.

We've been contracted by the *Engine City Times*, a small paper in the medium-sized city in the Midwest, Engine City, to build an online version of their newspaper. Engine City is a fine town and boasts a vibrant and active citizenry, who demand only the best from their local paper. It's up to us build a simple and usable website so the population can get their news online.

The site we'll create is a small newspaper website that will cover news, sports, politics, and obituaries and that will feature a political cartoon from a national cartoonist. We'd like to offer some newer web technologies, too, so the website will have an RSS feed with the latest news. As a way to make it easier to find older news, the site will also feature a simple keyword search tool.

We'll create a basic site with some content, but we'll leave it to the folks at the *Engine City Times* to fully populate the site with new stories.

So we can focus on the ExpressionEngine part of building a site, I've already done some of the legwork and created a design and the XHTML/ CSS templates. The templates I've created are filled with sample content that will be replaced and powered by ExpressionEngine.

Before we go any further, go ahead and download the templates from the book website.[1]

---

1. http://pragprog.com/titles/riexen

Figure 3.1: *Engine City Times* HOME PAGE

Once you've downloaded them, you should be able to open any of the templates in your web browser. Take a minute now to view them in both the browser and in your favorite text editor. Make yourself familiar with the XHTML and CSS.

3.1 *Engine City Times* Home Page

The *Engine City Times* home page, shown in Figure 3.1, is the first page the site visitor will see and provides an overview of the news. This template includes a Top Stories section with a lead article and three secondary articles. We plan to keep this very rigid and allow only four articles total to appear in this space.

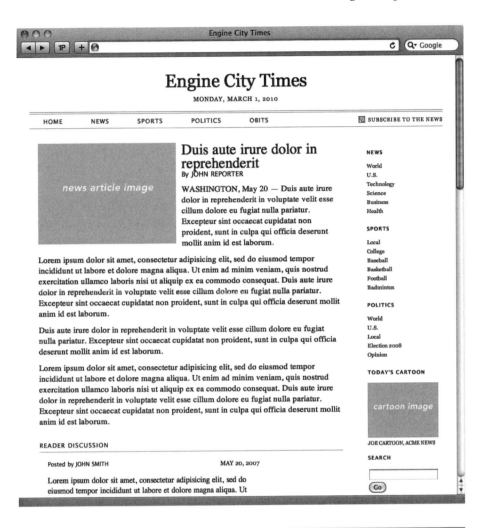

Figure 3.2: *Engine City Times* ARTICLE PAGE

Below the top stories is a Letters to the Editor section, where comments, letters, and emails from readers are shared. This section is limited to the three most recent letters.

The other elements on the page are global—they appear on every page on the website. This includes the masthead, the main navigation, and the topics navigation on the far right.

3.2 *Engine City Times* Article Page

The article page, as shown in Figure 3.2, on the preceding page, displays a full news article.

Engine City Times wants to be as open as possible and would like to encourage public debate and discussion of new stories. For this reason, the newspaper has decided to include the ability to comment on any news article posted to the website. The comments are below the article.

Below the comments section there is a three-column list of related articles. This section pulls in the most recent articles that are related by category or topic.

This template will also pull double duty as our generic content template. Since the main content area (where the article content lives) is very simple, we can co-opt this template for static pages, such as an About page or Contact page.

3.3 *Engine City Times* Category Page

There will be a category page for each of the main categories (News, Sports, Politics, and Obituaries) and also one for each subcategory listed on the far right of the page in Figure 3.3, on the next page.

The category pages will contain three recent and featured articles, in three columns along the top. Below this will be a list of other news articles in this category and then a selected image or cartoon.

3.4 Moving Forward

In the following chapters, we'll build out the entire website and learn some ExpressionEngine chops along the way.

We'll first learn how to configure ExpressionEngine (using the Control Panel) for the *Engine City Times* website. This will include setting site preferences and creating template groups, category groups, and status groups, as well as the templates, categories, and statuses that live in those groups. After that we'll start creating the templates and watch as the site slowly comes to life in our web browser.

We'll also learn how to display content in the template, including category lists and article comments, and how to limit content by status.

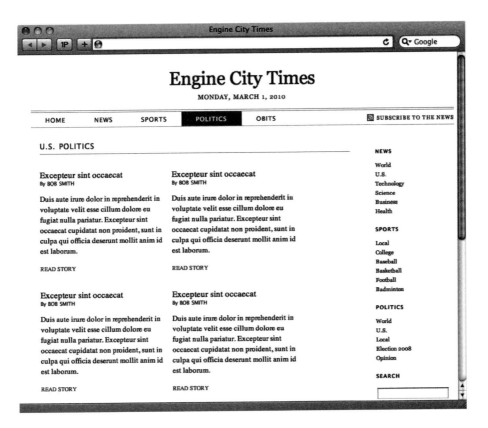

Figure 3.3: *Engine City Times* CATEGORY PAGE

Additionally, we'll add a couple of static pages and learn more about the Pages module in ExpressionEngine.

Finally, we'll tidy up our templates and make the site ready for some more advanced topics that we will cover in Part III of the book.

Chapter 4

Creating and Configuring the Site

With the numerous client meetings and conference calls out of the way, let's get started building the site for the *Engine City Times*.

Over the course of this chapter, we'll do the following:

- Set the site preferences
- Identify and create the different channels of the website
- Create custom channel fields for each channel
- Set up custom statuses to control the article creation workflow and give the newspaper editors the power to control which articles are published and which are not
- Add a category group and parent and child categories
- Create member groups and restrict access to certain aspects of the Control Panel

Let's get started.

4.1 Setting the Preferences

First, we'll learn how to edit the system preferences in ExpressionEngine. Although we'll alter only one of the many preferences, this is an important point of control in ExpressionEngine, because it allows us to affect every part of the front and back ends of our site.

Log back into the Control Panel, and navigate to the System Administration area by using the Admin button at the top, and then click General Configuration, which allows us to edit the settings for the entire site. What we're after is the setting called "Name of your site."

The name of our site is *Engine City Times*, so we'll want to replace the text in the field. When we start building our templates, we'll be able to call this preference as a variable. Instead of hard-coding the title of the site in the template, we'll just call the {site_name} variable, and it will output whatever we just put in the site name field.

Click Submit at the bottom to save the change to the site name.

4.2 Cleaning Up the Default Site

Let's clear our plate and give ourselves a fresh start. When we installed ExpressionEngine, we chose to also install the Agile Records default site. That was useful for poking around the software and learning how it works. Now we want to remove all the content and categories and then edit the channel that the installer created.

Removing the Default Templates

Head over to the Template Management section by clicking the Design button; select Templates and then Template Manager. Remove all the templates from the "news" group, *except* the index template (which ExpressionEngine won't let you delete anyway). We delete templates by clicking Delete in the far-right column of each template. ExpressionEngine will warn us that deleted templates cannot be undone. Click Delete to confirm.

Open the index template, clear the contents of it, and then save it; we end up with a blank template. As a last step, we'll rename the "news" template group to "site." Do this by selecting the template group and then clicking the Edit Group button. Change "news" to "site " and then click Update.

While we're in a destructive mood, let's completely delete both of the remaining template groups. Select a group from the far-left list, and then click the red Delete Group button at the top of the list of templates.

Deleting Content and Categories

Some other leftovers from installing the Agile Records site are a few entries and categories. When creating any new website, none of these will be of any use to us, so let's purge them all from the system.

Navigate to the Edit Channel Entries page by using the Content button and then clicking Edit. We see several content items listed here. To delete these, check the box to the far right of each item, and then choose Delete Selected from the selection list right below it. Click Submit and then Delete on the warning screen, and it's gone!

To access the categories, click the Admin button; then choose Channel Administration and then Categories. We see two category groups that contain two categories each. Click Delete Group next to each to delete the category group and all the categories inside.

Finally, let's delete the channels that ExpressionEngine created during the installation. Click Administration in the *breadcrumb*, which is the row of text links under the main button navigation that shows the current location, and a list of options should appear. From that list choose Channels under the Channel Administration section. To the far right, click Delete to remove the channels Information Pages and News.

Ah, now it's all nice and clean. We have a fresh start with Expression-Engine, with none of the cruft created during installation. With that done, let's move on to planning how we'll handle the website content in the Control Panel.

4.3 Representing the Content

In this section, we'll learn how to create and customize site channels using the Channel Management screen in the Administration section. Our main focus will be creating custom channel fields, which allow us to make the publish forms fit the amount and types of content on the *Engine City Times* website. After going through it together, I'll have you do some work on your own.

Let's get started with the site channels.

Engine City Times has four types of content on the site:

- News articles

- Letters to the editor

- Obituaries

- Static pages (About, Contact)

These are very large and distinct sections of the website, so it should be obvious that they all deserve their own channel within Expression-Engine. By giving each type of content its own channel, we create a separation between the content, which allows us to easily grant only

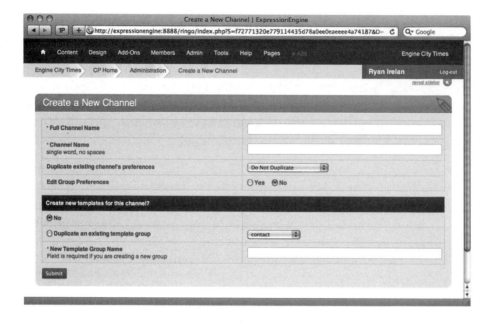

Figure 4.1: CREATING A NEW SITE CHANNEL CALLED NEWS ARTICLES

certain people access to different types of content (for example, only let the obit team add and edit the Obituaries channel, while only allowing news reporters access to the News Articles channel).

Another benefit of separating the content is that it becomes easier to enter content. If a reporter wants to add a news article, they simply add a new entry to the News Article channel. Each channel has its own publish form, and we will tailor each form to that specific content type. We'll create those in a few minutes.

Creating Site Channels

But first we need to create the channels in ExpressionEngine that will hold the content. Head back into the Control Panel, and click the Admin button; then select Channel Administration and then Channels (if you've been following along, this is where we left off). You should see no channels listed. If you do, you probably didn't remove the default channel (see Section 4.2, *Deleting Content and Categories*, on page 44).

Click the gray Create a New Channel button at the top right. To create this new channel, we need to give ExpressionEngine a few pieces information, including the full channel name and the short channel name.

The full name is a plain-English name that accurately describes what the content is. The channel name is a single-word name with no spaces (hyphens and underscores are permitted). Keep your naming conventions very simple and descriptive. Although obscure or coded names may make sense to you now, they may not to the person who comes after you to work on the site.

The first channel we'll create is News Articles. We'll use the full name "News Articles" and the short name "news_articles," as you see in Figure 4.1, on the preceding page. We don't want to duplicate any existing channel preferences (there are none), and we want Edit Group Preferences set to No. We will edit the full set of preferences after we've created the channel.

We also have the option of creating a new template for this channel. This will save us some time, so we'll take ExpressionEngine up on the offer.

Select "Duplicate an existing template group," and the group "site" should be selected by default since it's the only one available. This group has only the index template that we cleared earlier. Every template group has to have an index template, so this will make a great starting point.

Below that option there is an empty text field. Here we want to input the name of the template group we want ExpressionEngine to create. For the sake of consistency, I like to name my channels and corresponding template groups the same thing. So, input "news_articles" into the empty text field.

Review the form to make sure everything is correct, and then click Submit to create the News Articles channel.

Setting Channel Preferences

Now that we have our News Articles channel created, it's time to edit the channel preferences and do some fine-tuning. Click the Edit Preferences link.

Each channel has eight sets of preferences. Finely tuned control over channels in ExpressionEngine is fairly elaborate. We won't set all of the preferences right now, but instead we'll come back later to adjust some, as needed. We do, however, want to set up some basic preferences for the News Articles channel by doing the following:

- Enabling versioning

- Setting notification preferences

Enabling Versioning

Choose Versioning Preferences from the list of preferences by clicking it. The preferences should slide down and appear as shown in Figure 4.2, on the facing page. We want to enable versioning for this channel, so toggle the radio button to Yes.

When you enable versioning, ExpressionEngine tracks, by default, up to ten changes at once for every piece of content you create. You can track as many versions as you'd like, but in this situation, ten versions is enough. We think this is a great service to our client and the writers at *Engine City Times*, so we'll enable it. If, for some reason, a writer accidentally deletes a portion of their article copy, they can simply go back to the previous revision in ExpressionEngine, and it will be restored. Revisions to even hundreds of articles do not take up copious amount of space in the database, so it's a worthwhile feature to turn on.

Setting Notification Preferences

Now we want to edit the notification preferences for this channel so ExpressionEngine alerts us by email when certain actions take place.

Choose the Notification Preferences from the list of preferences by clicking it. It should slide up and display a few different settings.

Notification Preferences allow us to send email alerts whenever someone adds a new entry or new comment to the system. You should see three different settings; the first one is for entries and the last two are for comments. For now we only want to enable the settings for comments.

First, we will create a general list of comment notifications. Find "Enable recipient list below for comment notification" and toggle the radio button to Yes. Fill out the next field with at least one email address (you can add multiple email addresses by separating them with commas). These email addresses will receive a notification email every time someone leaves a new comment on any entry in the system. This is helpful for the Engine City Times because they have a few interns who

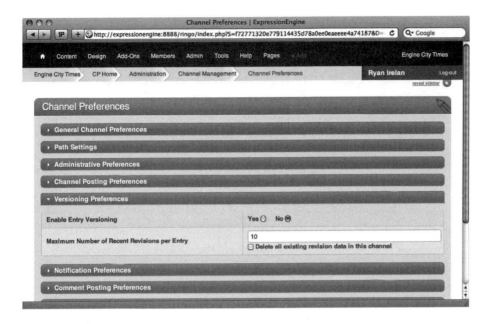

Figure 4.2: ENABLING ENTRY VERSIONING IN THE NEWS ARTICLES CHANNEL

are constantly monitoring comments to keep out off-topic or abusive comments. Adding your own email address for testing purposes will work just fine.

The last setting under Notification Preferences is to notify the author of an entry when a new comment is posted. Select the Yes radio button to enable this feature. Now, not only will the list of email addresses above get a notification for each new comment, but so will the author.

Once you have those preferences set, click Update and Finished.

Up to this point we've created our channels and set up the channel preferences. Let's move forward and create the fields we need to enter our content.

Creating Custom Channel Fields

We are now entering into a very powerful part of ExpressionEngine—the ability to create custom publish forms for any channel on our site. Not only are we creating a front-end form that appears in the user interface,

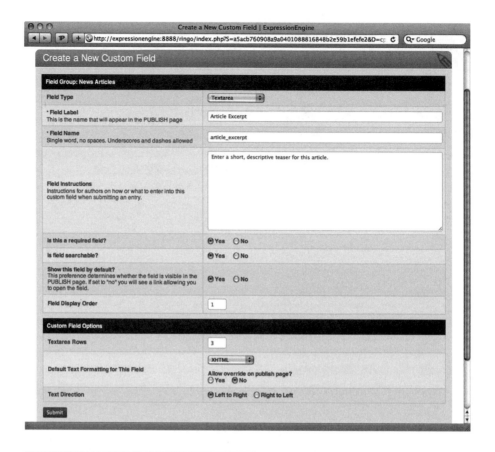

Figure 4.3: CREATING A NEW CUSTOM FIELD FOR THE NEWS ARTICLES
CHANNEL

but we're also customizing the type and amount of data we can store in
the database.

After saving the preferences in the previous section, we ended up at the
Channel Management screen. Click Administration in the breadcrumb
trail at the top, and then choose the Custom Fields option under Channel Administration.

There are two field groups that we neglected to delete during our cleanup. Quickly delete both field groups by clicking the Delete Field Group
text.

We want to create a new field group and customize it for our News Articles channel on the website. But before we do that, we need to decide what content we want to capture (and then later display on the website).

Flip back to the previous chapter, and take a look at the designs of the *Engine City Times* website. From looking at the design of the front page of the site and the article view page, we can see that we need space for the following:

- Article title
- Article excerpt or teaser
- Article body

ExpressionEngine requires a title for every entry, so that field is already created for us. The other two we'll create by clicking the gray Create a New Channel Field Group button.

The first step is to give the field group a name. As with previous steps, we want to choose a name that is simple, clear, and easily identifiable with the News Article channel of the website. Let's call it "News Articles." Enter that in the empty text field, and then click Submit.

To use the new field group, it has to be assigned to a channel. We will do that after we populate our new group with some fields.

Next to the name of our new group, click Add/Edit Custom Fields, and then click the gray Create a New Custom Field button. Since ExpressionEngine already provides us with the title field, we only need to create two custom fields: Article Excerpt and Article Body.

Let's first create the Article Excerpt field. The type of field we want is a textarea because we're entering a paragraph of text and a text input field will not be enough room. Choose Textarea from the list.

We want to call it "Article Excerpt," so we'll input that into the first field, Field Label. The second field has to be a single word with no spaces, so let's use "article_excerpt." We can optionally give the user some instructions for this field. These will appear just above the field itself. Let's add something simple: "Enter a short, descriptive teaser for this article. This will appear on the front page of the website."

Set this field as required and searchable. By requiring the field, it will have to be filled in order to publish the article. Opening this field up to search will allow visitors to the newspaper site to search on its text using the search functionality we'll build later.

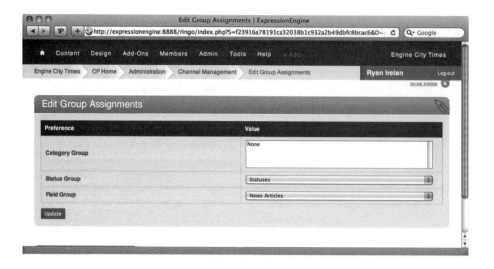

Figure 4.4: Assigning the field group to the News Articles channel

We want this field to be shown by default, and finally we will set it to be first in the display order.

Let's shorten up the textarea rows to 3 as a visual reminder to the user that this is an excerpt and should be short.

The Default Text Formatting setting for this field should remain as XHTML. This means that ExpressionEngine will create XHTML for the entry, so the writer doesn't have to create p tags around paragraphs. We also want to disallow overriding the formatting on the publish form so that the writers are unable to alter the formatting type, which could affect how the content displays on the website. Finally, we can leave the text direction as is.

Click Submit to create the new field.

Go ahead and create the second custom field: Article Body. We want to name it "article_body," give it short instructions, give it a Field Type value of Textarea, and then give it all of the other settings we used in the previous field. Set Field Display Order to 2 so this field displays after the Article Excerpt field we created a moment ago.

Assigning the Field Group

One last detail before we finish up with this section of the site: remember earlier when I mentioned that we would not be able to use this custom field group until we assign it a channel? Well, let's do that now.

Navigate to the Channel Management screen (click Administration in the breadcrumb trail, and then choose Channels from the list under Channel Administration). We can see the News Articles channel (Figure 4.4, on the preceding page). To the right, click the Edit Group Assignments link. Here we assign our newly created field group to the News Articles channel.

Choose News Articles from the drop-down menu, and click Update. Now we're all set!

Up to this point you should have created a News Articles site channel, adjusted the site preferences, and created the custom fields needed to add the news article content to ExpressionEngine.

On Your Own

We just walked through how to create site channels and custom channel fields for the News Articles channel. We still have two more channels in this website: Letters to Editor and Obituaries. Rather than walk through creating those, this is a good time for me to hand it off to you to practice what you've learned so far.

Here's some information on the remaining two channels that you'll find helpful.

Letters to Editor

You might consider using the following names for the site channel and template group:

- *Short name*: letters_to_editor

- *Template group name*: letters_to_editor

To save yourself some time in setting up the preferences, try using the "Duplicate existing channel's preferences" option when creating the channel. Here's what it will look like:

What fields do you think we need to create? Take a look at the designs in the previous chapter. The Letters to Editor channel appears on the bottom of the front page.

Here are my suggestions (full name/short name/formatting):

- Author Name/author_name/no formatting
- Letter Copy/letter_copy/XHTML formatting

Obituaries

For the channel name, you might consider the following:

- *Short name*: obits
- *Template group name*: obits

Again, use an existing channel's preferences to save yourself some time.

Obituaries appear in their own channel on the site. They contain two pieces of information: a title (the name of the deceased) and the text of the obituary. Remember that ExpressionEngine automatically generates a title field for every channel because it is required. Therefore, you have to create only one field for this channel. I recommend the following:

- Obit Copy/obit_copy/XHTML formatting

After you create the channel fields, don't forget to assign them to the proper channel!

Now that we have set up ExpressionEngine to handle our website content using custom fields, let's move forward and configure ExpressionEngine to handle different pieces of content in different ways using custom statuses.

4.4 Controlling Content with Custom Statuses

Custom statuses are a powerful way to control how and where content appears on a website. In this section, we'll explore ExpressionEngine's support for custom statuses, create our own, and discuss how they will help define the content publishing workflow.

The News Articles channel of *Engine City Times* will have many different articles, but we need a way to mark certain articles as featured. If you look back at the design, you'll notice the front page has one featured top story, followed by three other top stories that are less prominent.

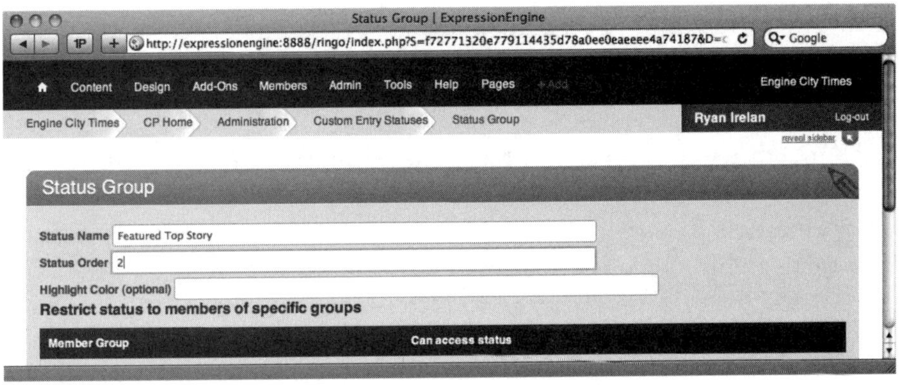

Figure 4.5: CREATING CUSTOM STATUSES FOR THE NEWS ARTICLES CHANNEL

We could let ExpressionEngine set the latest story as the featured top story, but that would remove a lot of editorial control from the newspaper editors. We need to tell ExpressionEngine which news articles to feature, and then later we'll call those featured articles in our template.

The way we give the *Engine City Times* editors control over featured top stories is through statuses. By default every piece of content we create in ExpressionEngine has a status of either "open" or "closed." Open means that the article is appearing on the front end of the website. Closed means it is not. You can alter this in your templates, but that's how it works by default.

ExpressionEngine also gives us the ability to specify our own statuses, called *custom entry statuses*. We can create as many statuses as we'd like, and then in the templates we are able to control which content is displayed based on the status.

Creating Statuses

For the *Engine City Times* website, we need to create two statuses in addition to the Open and Closed statuses that ExpressionEngine requires.

The first status we will call Top Story, and this will allow an article with this status to appear in the Top Stories section of the front page of the website. The second status we need is Featured Top Story, which will determine which news article displays at the very top of the Top Stories section (the largest article). Let's create those statuses now.

From the Admin button, select Channel Administration, and then click Custom Status Groups. You should see a group called Statuses (Figure 4.5, on the preceding page). We'll use this status group for our other channels in the site, because they don't need the special statuses that we're giving the news articles.

Click the gray Create New Status Group button at the top right, and then name the status group "News Articles." Click Submit, and we're brought back to the Status Groups page.

You'll notice that our new group already shows two statuses, but we didn't add any! This is because ExpressionEngine requires that the statuses "open" and "closed" be in every status group and automatically adds them for us.

Click the Add/Edit Statuses link. Use the gray Create a New Status button to create a status called "Top Story." We'll give it a Status Order value of 1 and leave the Highlight Color field blank. Click Submit to add the status. Let's do the same for the status Featured Top Story.

Even though we told ExpressionEngine to display Top Story first and Featured Top Story second, the statuses are now in this order: open, Top Story, closed, Featured Top Story.

The statuses "open" and "closed" already had the order 1 and 2, so when we created our custom statuses with those same order numbers, ExpressionEngine ordered statuses with the same order number alphabetically. This isn't a problem because we'll just renumber the statuses so they appear in our desired order of Top Story, Featured Top Story, open, closed. Click Update to save the changes. To do this, click into each status, and adjust the order number (Figure 4.6, on the next page).

You should now have a News Articles status group that contains four statuses: Featured Top Story, Top Story, open, and closed.

Assigning Status Groups

Before we forget, let's assign this new status group to our News Articles channel. On the Edit Group Assignments screen for the News Articles channel, we choose the News Articles status group.

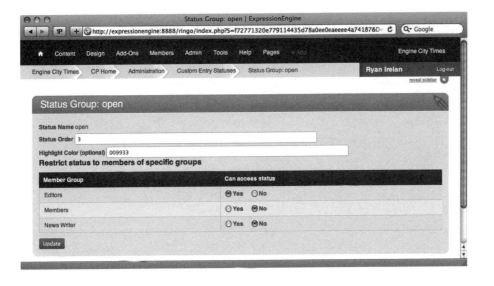

Figure 4.6: CHANGING THE ORDER OF THE STATUSES

Now when the editors at *Engine City Times* want to decide which stories are top stories and which one is featured, they simply adjust the status of any article in the system.

Using custom statuses, we created the first part of a very powerful workflow system for publishing content to the newspaper website. With that out of the way, we can now focus on categories and then finally wrap up with creating the members and member groups to round out the site configuration in ExpressionEngine.

4.5 Working with Categories

In ExpressionEngine you can assign every piece of content a category. You use categories to organize content in some sort of taxonomy or as a way to control where and how content is displayed on a website. In this section, we'll learn how to create categories and category groups.

For the *Engine City Times* website, we're going to use categories in their simplest form—as a way to organize content. The only part in the site that will use categories is the News Articles channel. Take a look at the site design again, and you'll see a list of categories on the far right.

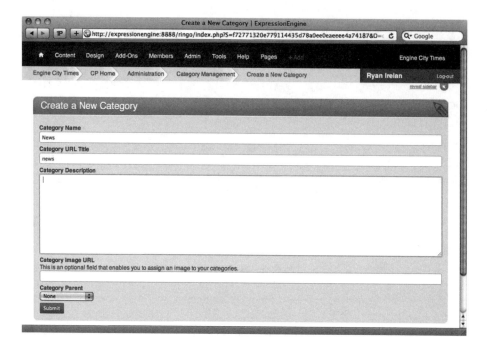

Figure 4.7: CREATING CATEGORIES FOR THE NEWS ARTICLES CHANNEL

News, Sports, and Politics are the top-level categories, and those underneath are subcategories.

Just like statuses, categories are organized into groups. This makes it easy to assign an entire set of categories to one channel of the website.

We're going to have three parent categories, and each parent will have multiple child categories. We'll set all of this up through the ExpressionEngine Control Panel.

Creating Categories

The first step is to create a new group for our News Article categories. Click the Admin button, and then select Categories under Channel Administration. There aren't any categories or category groups, so click the gray Create a New Category Group button to create a new group.

Let's name the group "News Articles." You'll notice that there is some information there about who can edit and delete categories. We can safely ignore this for now, because we'll be dealing with members and permission in the next section of this chapter.

Click Submit to create the new group. We're now ready to begin adding the categories to the group. We'll do a few together, and then you'll do the rest on your own.

Click the Add/Edit Categories and then the gray Create a New Category button. You will see an entry form like that shown in Figure 4.7, on the facing page. We're going to first create the parent categories and then their children.

Let's start with the News category. The Category Name value will be "News." We'll let ExpressionEngine create the Category URL Title value. We will leave the Category Description value and leave the Category Image URL value blank. Since this is a parent category, the Category Parent drop-down should be None. Click Submit to add the category.

Creating a child category is the same as done earlier, but we'll assign it to the parent category News. Here are the child categories of News:

- World
- U.S.
- Technology
- Science
- Business
- Health

After adding these categories and assigning them the parent News, they should appear under News on the Category Management screen.

If you have a keen eye, you'll notice that the categories are not in the same order in which we entered them (see Figure 4.8, on the next page). By default, ExpressionEngine orders the categories alphabetically unless we tell it otherwise.

The editors at *Engine City Times* have a specific order to their newspaper sections in the print version of their paper and would like to replicate that on the website. To do a custom sort order, use the up and down arrows to organize the categories just like they were listed earlier. When you have completed reordering the categories, click Update to save them. Your list should now be in the order that it appears in the site design.

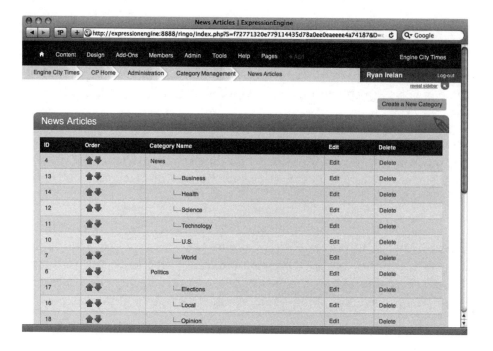

Figure 4.8: PARENT AND CHILD CATEGORIES LISTED ALPHABETICALLY

On Your Own

We still have two more parent categories and their children to enter into ExpressionEngine. We did the first set of categories together, so go ahead and do the rest on your own. Start with the parent category, and then create and assign its children. You can find a complete list of the categories in the static templates you downloaded from the book website.

When you're finished, your list of categories for the News Articles group should all be in the same order as in the design in the previous chapter.

One thing to note while you're creating the other categories is that ExpressionEngine requires that the category URL be unique across all categories. This is so if you go to that URL, you get to the correct category (for example, World News instead of World Politics). If you get a warning that the category URL already exists, simply append _politics (as an example) to the category name (resulting in world_politics), and you should be all set.

Now that we have the categories entered and organized, we need to assign this category group to the News Articles channel. Navigate to the Channel Management page, and Choose Edit Group Assignments for News Articles. Select the category group News Articles, and then click Update.

With the categories created, we are almost finished with setting up the site inside the Control Panel. The final step is to create authors and members so the writers and editors can access the site.

4.6 Creating Authors and Members

In this section, we will learn the basics of member and group management using ExpressionEngine's Member module. The Member module provides us with everything from member account creation to management to restricting a member's access to site content and Control Panel functionality through permissions.

The newspaper editors wanted all of their writers and editors to have access to ExpressionEngine. However, not everyone should have the same type of access. For example, one writer should not be able to edit the work of another, and editors should have access to everyone's writing. We could get fairly granular with the permissions, but for this site we want to keep it manageable and simple to build.

In ExpressionEngine we are able to restrict members to only a single channel and then restrict what they can do in that channel (for example, add new articles but not edit others). We will set up the workflow so that all articles submitted by the writers will be set to the status of "closed," and then an editor at the newspaper will come behind them and either have the writer make changes or approve the articles to be published to the website by setting the status to "open."

Creating Member Groups

By creating member groups, we can easily assign permissions to many people at once by assigning a specific set of permissions to the group.

To create a new member group, click the Members button at the top of the Control Panel, and choose Member Groups from the list.

We see that ExpressionEngine has already created some of the groups for us, but unfortunately we don't currently have any use for them.

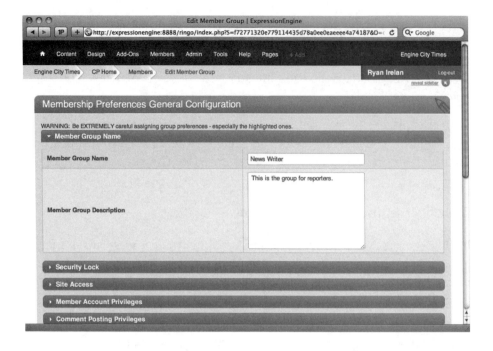

Figure 4.9: CREATING A MEMBER GROUP FOR THE NEWS WRITERS

Since most of them are default groups that cannot be deleted, we'll just ignore them all for now.

Click the gray Create a New Member Group button.

Don't get scared off by the long list of member preferences on the page. ExpressionEngine offers a powerful set of tools to fine-tune member permissions, but we're not going to set them all, and we'll walk through the process together.

The first step is to name the group. We want to first create a group for the team of writers who work in the News section of the newspaper. We'll call this group "News Writers" and give it a brief description: "This is the group for reporters" (see Figure 4.9).

For security reasons, ExpressionEngine gives every new group the most restrictive permissions. This keeps someone from creating a new group and forgetting to revoke permissions. Everything is locked down by default, and you have to explicitly grant access. Because of this, we won't go through every preference listed. Those that don't apply to the

News Writers group are turned off, so there are no worries about them having access they shouldn't.

We want to change the following preferences for this group:

- *Control Panel Access*: Switch this to Yes. We want the writers to be able to log in and write their news articles. Additionally, grant access to the Content section, Publish page, and Edit page (listed as "CONTENT section", "CONTENT: Publish", and "CONTENT: Edit"). Everything else should be set to No. We want the writers to be able to access the content section, create new articles, and edit their own articles.

- *Channel Assignment*: Grant the group access to post and edit entries in the News Articles channel.

After we have those permissions set, click Submit, which returns us to the Member Groups page. Our new group appears in the list in red lettering. This denotes that the group has Control Panel access.

Restricting Article Status

One of the requirements from the newspaper is that the writers—no matter which section they write for—are only able to submit articles to ExpressionEngine that have a status of "closed." Only editors are allowed to set articles to "open" and have them published to the site.

The first step in setting up this workflow for the News Writers group is to go to the Channel Management screen and click Edit Preferences for the News Articles channel. Click Administrative Preferences, set Default Status to "closed," and click Update and Finished to save the changes. Now every new article that is created by the writers will have a status of "closed." We have one more step remaining to really lock this down.

Right now the writers still have ability to change the status of an article. We want to revoke that privilege.

Navigate to the Administration screen, and choose Custom Status Groups. Click Add/Edit Statuses next to the News Articles status group. Click the Edit text next to the "open" status. At the bottom you'll see an extra preference that wasn't there before. We had to first assign this group permissions to access the Publish and Edit areas of the Control Panel before this ability to restrict status to News Writers group would appear.

Change the Can Access Status option for News Writers to No, and click Update. We'll need to do the same thing for the Top Story and Featured Top Story statuses. Now when a news writer creates a new article, it will automatically have the status of "closed," and the writer will not be able to change that status.

Creating the Editors Group

Before I give you some work to do on your own, let's first create the Editors group and assign it the appropriate permissions. In the previous section, we limited the writers in the News Articles group to a status of "closed" for every article they created in ExpressionEngine. The members of the Editors group (the newspaper editors) are the people in charge of setting a article from "closed" to "open" or Top Story or Featured Top Story. The editors are the final clearance point on what gets published to the *Engine City Times* website and what doesn't—just like in the print newspaper.

Like we did with the previous group, navigate to the Member Groups page, and click the gray Create a New Member Group button to create a new member group.

We're going to name this group "Editors" and give it a short description that reads "Editors at Engine City Times." Remember that Expression-Engine creates a very restrictive set of permissions by default, so we'll need to loosen them up slightly to give our editors their editorial power.

We want to change the following preferences for this group:

- *Control Panel Access*: Switch this to Yes. We want the editors to be able to log in and edit or approve the articles their team of writers submitted. Additionally, grant access to the Content section, Publish page, and Edit page. Everything else should be set to No. We want the editors to be able to access the content section, create new articles or edit their own articles, as well as articles from the team of writers.

- *Channel Posting Privileges*: This is where the editors get some of their power. The writers are not allowed to view or edit entries by other writers, but we want the editors to have that ability. Set everything to Yes *except* the last two items, which are in red.

- *Channel Assignment*: We want to grant the editors permission to post and edit entries in all three channels.

Click Submit to save the new Editors group.

Up to this point you should have created two member groups: News Writers and Editors.

On Your Own

Together we created the News Writers and Editors member groups. We still need to create groups for the teams that work on obituaries and letters to the editor. On your own, using the previous steps as an example, create these two groups in ExpressionEngine. They should both have the same permissions as the News Writers group.

When you've completed creating the groups, add a member to each group. Using a fake name and personal information will be fine for now. After you create the group members, log in with the different members, and see how the permissions affect what ExpressionEngine displays to the user in the Control Panel.

4.7 What We Learned

So far in our *Engine City Times* project, we set up ExpressionEngine to handle the website content using template groups, custom channel fields, and categories. We also created two custom statuses and set some strict user permissions, creating a workflow that allows the newspaper editors to tightly control what does and does not get published to the website.

Now that we have the Control Panel set up, we can begin creating some of the front-end templates, which we'll build in the next chapter.

Chapter 5

Making the Pages

In the previous chapter, we set up ExpressionEngine to handle all of the content of our *Engine City Times* website. In this chapter, we'll reap the benefits of the work we've done and begin to see the *Engine City Times* website come together. We'll focus on creating the templates and on using ExpressionEngine to display content, list categories, and add commenting functionality to articles.

We've made a lot of progress so far, but there is still work to do to bring the website to life.

5.1   Building Out the Home Page

Let's first change things up a bit and start off with a little DIY work for you. Before we can jump in and create our templates, it would make sense to have some content to display. We could certainly create the templates without content, but it would be a challenge knowing whether the code we're writing is actually working correctly.

Creating Placeholder Content

For the front page, we need to create four news articles. We need one article to be a Featured Top Story and the rest to be Top Story articles. Click the Content button, click Publish, and then choose News Articles. This will bring you to the news articles publish form, as shown in Figure 5.1, on the next page. Give the article a title, excerpt, and body. You can see that I'm using a fake title and some fake Latin text for the news copy. Since this is just to help us out while coding the templates, it's not important that this content makes sense or is even real. The people

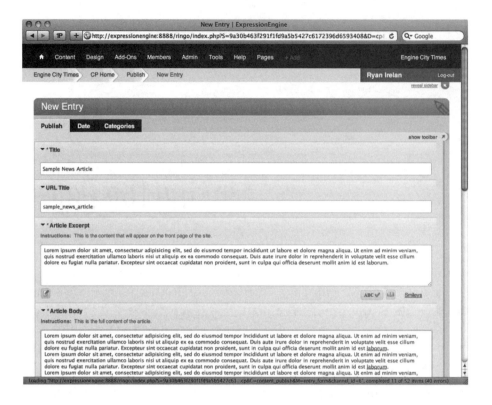

Figure 5.1: ADDING SAMPLE CONTENT TO THE NEWS ARTICLE SECTION

at *Engine City Times* will do all of the data entry, so we just have to put enough in to help us build the site.

After you entered the content, click over to the Categories tab, and choose World, which is nested under News. We want to assign all the sample content to the same category so that later in the chapter we can easily build the category template. (Since all of the category pages use the same template, once we build one, we've built them all.)

Click over to the Options tab. Here we need to set the status of the article. You'll remember from the previous chapter that we created two custom statuses for new articles: Top Story and Featured Top Story. Let's make this article the one that appears at the very top of the site (there can be only one) by assigning it the Featured Top Story status. Click Submit to add the article and publish it on the site.

On your own, create three Top Story articles using the news articles publish form. Don't forget to use the proper status!

When you've completed creating the placeholder content, you should have four articles listed when viewing the Edit screen. Three articles should have a status of Top Story and one Featured Top Story.

The last set of placeholder content we have to create is for the Letters to the Editor section. This section appears at the bottom of the home page and contains three very short letter from readers, displayed in their entirety. Navigate to the letters publish form using the Content button. Give each letter a title, author name, and letter copy. Letters don't have any categories or custom statuses, so we can fill out the form and just click Submit to save the letter and publish it to the website.

With those three letters created, we should now have seven pieces of content—four news articles and three letters to the editor—listed on the Edit screen.

Starting Static

Open the directory of *Engine City Times* templates you downloaded in Chapter 3, *What We're Building*, on page 37. Find the img directory, and upload it to the root of your website on the server. This directory contains a few images we need for the site.

With that uploaded, open the template template-home.html in your favorite text editor. Using the Design button, go to the Template Manager. Copy the static template—in its entirety—and paste it into the index template under the site group in ExpressionEngine. Click Update to save the changes to the template.

Open the site in your browser (or click the gray View Rendered Template button). You'll notice that the template changes are there, but there is no styling. Why? Because we haven't added the CSS that makes page look nice. Let's do that now.

There are two ways to manage CSS files for ExpressionEngine-powered websites. There is the traditional way of having the CSS file live somewhere on the server and just referenced in the head element of the HTML document. With ExpressionEngine you can also put your CSS in a template, which keeps it together with the rest of your template code.

We didn't create a CSS template in the previous chapter, so let's do that now. Navigate to the site template group in the Template Manager, and create a new empty template named site_css. Choose a Template Type value of CSS. Click Create to add the new template.

In the downloaded directory of site template files, open core.css, which is located in the css directory. Copy the entire contents of the file into the newly created site_css template, and save it.

There's one more step left before the styles will be applied to the index template. We need to link the stylesheet template in the index template. Open the index template, and find this line near the top:

EngineCityTimes/template-home.html

```
<link rel="stylesheet" href="css/screen/main.css"
type="text/css" media="screen" />
```

Replace the value of the href parameter with this ExpressionEngine-specific code:

```
{stylesheet=site/site_css}
```

The new CSS link should look like this:

MakingthePages/template-home-ee.html

```
<link rel="stylesheet" href="{stylesheet=site/site_css}"
type="text/css" media="screen" />
```

Reload the home page of the site in your web browser, and you should now see the page fully rendered and looking just like Figure 5.2, on the next page.

Lighting Up the Page

Now that we have the entire template in ExpressionEngine (static content and all), we can begin *lighting up*—turning the content from static to dynamic—the template using content from the ExpressionEngine database. We'll do this one small section at a time, starting with the Featured Top Story.

Bringing the Featured Top Story to Life

The Featured Top Story consists of four parts: title, author, content, and link to the full article. We'll pull all of this information out of ExpressionEngine using one tag pair:

```
{exp:channel:entries} {/exp:channel:entries}
```

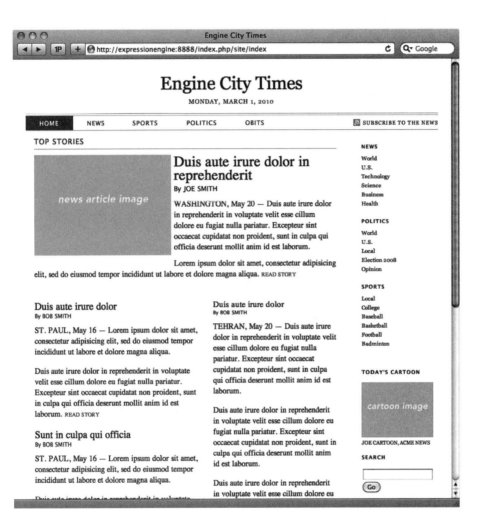

Figure 5.2: VIEWING THE SITE HOME PAGE WITH CSS INCLUDED

Find this chunk of code in the index template that controls the display of the Featured Top Story:

`EngineCityTimes/template-home.html`

```
<div id="lead-article">
 <img src="img/news-article-image.png"
  alt="Image Alt Here" />
 <h4>Duis aute irure dolor in reprehenderit</h4>
 <h5><span class="by">By</span> Joe Smith</h5>
 <p>WASHINGTON, May 20 &mdash; Duis aute irure dolor
in reprehenderit in voluptate velit esse
cillum dolore eu fugiat nulla pariatur. Excepteur
sint occaecat cupidatat non proident,
sunt in culpa qui officia deserunt mollit
anim id est laborum.</p>
<p>Lorem ipsum dolor sit amet, consectetur adipisicing elit,
sed do eiusmod tempor incididunt ut labore
et dolore magna aliqua.</p>

<p><a href="#" class="read_story"
>Read Story</a></p>
</div><!-- END #lead-article -->
```

We'll start by wrapping all of the content in the lead-article div with a basic ExpressionEngine Channel Entries tag pair:

```
{exp:channel:entries channel=""}
{/exp:channel:entries}
```

We want to enhance it slightly using some parameters. To the tag add the limit parameter with a value of 1 because we want only one Top Featured Story to appear at a time. Also add the disable parameter, and give it a value of pagination. This tells ExpressionEngine to not make the queries necessary to create pagination since we're not using it on this page. It's a simple way to optimize your template and make it load faster.[1]

You'll remember from the previous chapter that we set up Expression-Engine to allow the newspaper editors to use statuses to determine which news articles are tagged as Top Stories and which is the Featured Top Story. To make sure we're pulling the proper content, we also have to add the status parameter to the tag pair. We want the latest entry with the status of Featured Top Story, so make that the value of the status parameter. Finally, we need to give the channel parameter

---

1. See Chapter 9, *Advanced Templating*, on page 137 for more on template optimization.

the value of news_articles, which is the ExpressionEngine section from which we're pulling the content.

Your tag pair should now look like this:

```
{exp:channel:entries channel="news_articles"
limit="1" disable="pagination"
status="Featured Top Story"}
```

...

```
{/exp:channel:entries}
```

With the Channel Entries tag pair all set, let's replace the static content with ExpressionEngine variables that will pull in the content from the database. The tags we use are just the short names of the fields we created in the previous chapter. For this chunk of content, we will use {title} and {article_excerpt}. We'll populate the author byline using the {author} variable that ExpressionEngine makes available for every entry.

Place these variables in their proper places, replacing the static content in the template. That part of your template should look like this:

MakingthePages/template-home-ee.html

```
<div id="lead-article">
 {exp:channel:entries channel="news_articles"
 limit="1" disable="pagination"
 status="Featured Top Story"}

<img src="img/news-article-image.png" alt="" />
<h4>{title}</h4>
<h5><span class="by">By </span> {author}</h5>
{article_excerpt}
 <p>
      <a href="{title_permalink="news_articles/view"}"
class="read_story">Read Story</a></p>
 {/exp:channel:entries}
 </div><!-- END #lead-article -->
```

Besides the article image, which we'll ignore for now and come back to later, the only thing left to light up is the Read Story link that leads you to the full article. There are several different types of links you could create, but for our purposes we want the link to have the article title in the URL.

We'll use the {title_permalink} single variable and specify what template group and template the link should point to. We want to use a template that will show the entire article (more on that in Section 5.4, *Building Out the Article Template*, on page 83). Let's assume the template will be named "view." We'll want to create the *permalink*, the unique URL where this article will live, like so:

`MakingthePages/template-home-ee.html`

```
<p>
        <a href="{title_permalink="news_articles/view"}"
class="read_story">Read Story</a></p>
```

This variable will render a link that contains the article title at the end, preceded by the news_articles template group and view template.[2] We'll make that URL work shortly.

That's it for the Featured Top Story. Now we need to light up the rest of the top stories.

Let's review where we are. Up to this point you should have pasted in the static home page template and created a CSS template with the site CSS. Finally, you should have coded the Featured Top Story at the top of the home page of the *Engine City Times* website.

Secondary Top Stories

The secondary top stories appear in two columns below the Featured Top Story. The left column contains two stories, and the right column contains just one. This presents a slight challenge because we have to be smart about how we pull this content in from ExpressionEngine without breaking the page layout. We'll do each side separately and add a special parameter that will ensure we have unique content on both sides.

The left column contains two featured news articles, so we want to wrap it in an Channel Entries tag pair just like we did previously. The only difference this time is we set a different value for the status parameter and for the limit parameter. The status parameter value should be Top Story so we pull in the latest stories set as top stories. Set the limit parameter to 2 so we display only two stories on the left.

Use the same variables as we did on the Featured Top Story to light up the content. Since ExpressionEngine will loop through all entries based on the parameters, you need only one of the blocks of markup.

---

2. Your exact URL will look different, but here's an example: http://example.com/index. php/news_articles/view/sample_news_article/.

Your final code for displaying both top stories should look like this:

MakingthePages/template-home-ee.html

```
{exp:channel:entries channel="news_articles"
limit="2" disable="pagination" status="Top Story"}
<h4>{title}</h4>
<h5><span class="by">By </span> {author}</h5>
{article_excerpt}
<p><a href="{title_permalink="news_articles/view"}"
class="read_story">Read Story</a></p>
{/exp:channel:entries}
```

Save the changes to the template, and then view the site home page in your browser. Two articles from the ExpressionEngine database should appear in place of the static content that was there. The Read Story link should point to a URL that has the title in it. If everything looks good, let's move on to the single story that populates the right column.

The right column presents us with another challenge. If we just put in the same parameters as the left side, with the only change being limiting it to one single article, we'd see the same article on the right that is listed first on the left. So, how do we get around this?

The key is to use a parameter called offset. This parameter allows us to display an entry that is not the most recent but, for example, the latest minus 2. Add the Channel Entries tag pair to the right side, and replace the static content with the entry variables just like we did with the first two sets of content. The parameters should change, so we display only one story and then add the offset parameter and assign it a value of 2.

Your code should look like this:

MakingthePages/template-home-ee.html

```
{exp:channel:entries channel="news_articles"
disable="pagination" limit="1"
status="Top Story" offset="2"}
<h4>{title}</h4>
<h5><span class="by">By </span> {author}</h5>
{article_excerpt}
<p><a href="{title_permalink="news_articles/view"}"
class="read_story">Read Story</a></p>
{/exp:channel:entries}
```

Save the updated template, and then reload the site home page to view your changes. You should see all three top stories in their proper place—two on the left and one on the right. For an example of what your home page should look like, see Figure 5.3, on the following page.

Figure 5.3: VIEWING THE TOP STORIES ON THE HOME PAGE

Letters to the Editor

The last part of the home page content that we need to build out is the Letters to the Editor section at the very bottom of the page. This section contains three short letters from the newspaper readers. It includes a title, an author, and the letter copy. The entire letter is published on the front page, so there's no link to read more.

To display the letters content, we'll use the same Channel Entries tag pair as before but give the channel parameter the value of letters_to_editor so that we're pulling content from the Letters to Editor channel in ExpressionEngine. Since there are three letters displayed at one time, we want to use a value of 3 for the limit parameter. This will display the three most recently added letters. The Channel Entries tag pair should now look like this:

```
{exp:channel:entries
channel="letters_to_editor" limit="3"}
...
{/exp:channel:entries}
```

Looking at the HTML in the template, we notice that each letter is contained in its own div with a unique id. These ids reference CSS, which controls how the letters are presented on the page—in three columns, one letter per column. This presents a small challenge when dynamically pulling in content from ExpressionEngine because it wants to just pull it all in without regard for layout. Our goal is to use one entry tag pair to pull in all three letters. To accomplish this, we need to use an ExpressionEngine variable called switch. This variable rotates through different values as ExpressionEngine displays each entry on the page. We want to place the switch variable in the id parameter of the div that contains the letter and give it the values of the ids, separated by a pipe (|) character.

For this example, the switch variable will look like this:

```
{switch="lcol|mcol|rcol"}
```

This tells ExpressionEngine to rotate through each of the values—in order—for each entry that it displays. Since we're displaying only three entries, it'll use each value once. If we were displaying six entries, it would use each value twice (allowing us to create two rows of three columns).

The final code in your template for the Letters to Editor channel should look like this:

`MakingthePages/template-home-ee.html`

```
{exp:channel:entries channel="letters_to_editor"
limit="3"}
<div id="{switch="lcol|mcol|rcol"}">
 <h4>{title}</h4>
 <h5><span class="by">From</span> {author_name}</h5>
 {letter_copy}
</div>
{/exp:channel:entries}
```

We only need one of the markup blocks because ExpressionEngine will loop through and create all three for us. Save the template, and reload the home page to see your changes. It should look similar to the screenshot in Figure 5.4, on the next page.

With the major content pieces now being pulled from the database using ExpressionEngine, let's switch to the category list on the far-right column of the page and learn how to make a list of categories to display.

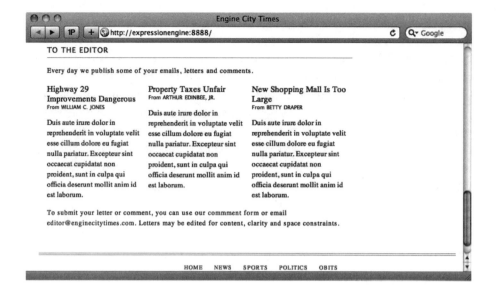

Figure 5.4: Dynamically displaying the letters to the editor using ExpressionEngine

5.2 Displaying the Categories

On the side of every page on the *Engine City Times* website there is a vertical list containing the parent and child categories for all news articles. All of the categories link to a category template (which we'll build at the end of this chapter) and are organized by parent categories. Look at the HTML, and you'll see that this is just a nested unordered list. The markup is straightforward, and the CSS does most of the heavy lifting to make the list appear styled and not like a default nested unordered list.

ExpressionEngine offers a convenient way to display nested categories —where the parent category is followed by its children—like those we have for the news articles. It's a tag pair for displaying categories, and it looks like this:

```
{exp:channel:categories channel="news_articles"}
...
{/exp:channel:categories}
```

This tag pair will output a nested unordered list with an id and class of nav_categories. Since our template is also coded using a nested unordered list, displaying the categories is going to be very simple. We just want to add two parameters to the Channel Categories tag pair and then link up each category so it points to the category view template.

The style parameter sets whether the categories are displayed in a nested unordered list or in a linear fashion (no markup at all). The values you can pass this parameter are nested and linear. (If you use the Channel Categories tag pair and do not specify a style, ExpressionEngine defaults to a nested display. Technically, we could just leave this parameter out for this example, but I find it good form to include it so the behavior of the ExpressionEngine tag is clear.)

We also want to include the id parameter, which will assign the unordered list a custom id. We need to use the id of category-nav, which will reference styles in our CSS. By doing this, we override the default id of nav_categories. Now our Channel Categories tag pair looks like this:

```
{exp:channel:categories channel="news_articles"
style="nested" id="category-nav"}
...
{/exp:channel:categories}
```

The only thing left is to place the proper variables between the tag so the category names appear and they link up to category pages. The variable we want to use is {category_name}, and we'll wrap it in an anchor link and use the path variable to set the URL to point to the news_articles template group and the page; template, which we'll create later. Your code for displaying the newspaper categories should now look like this:

MakingthePages/template-home-ee.html

```
{exp:channel:categories channel="news_articles"
 style="nested" id="category-nav"}
<a href="{path=news_articles/page}">{category_name}</a>
{/exp:channel:categories}
```

Before the category link will work properly, we need to tweak one setting in the global preferences, which you can access under the Channel Administration section of the Administration page (click Admin and choose Channel Administration and then Global Preferences). The first preference listed asks, "Use Category URL Titles in Links?" Select Yes, and then save the change by clicking Submit.

What we did was tell ExpressionEngine to use a underscored version of the category titles in the category page URLs instead of the default category ID. This method produces readable URLs that are not only easier to remember but much friendlier for search engine optimization efforts.

Reload the site home page, and you should now see a perfectly styled list of all the categories in the *Engine City Times* website.

5.3 Embedding Reusable Code

Before we go further and build out the rest of the site templates, let's first do some legwork that will make building and maintaining the templates easier. Some of the items on the front page of the site—the categories list, main navigation, document header, and so on—are also used elsewhere. We're going to break the template up into chunks and create several smaller templates that we can just include in any template in the site. The goal here is to never duplicate code in different templates.

In ExpressionEngine-speak, this method of reusing code is called *template embedding*, and the global variable {embed} is used to include one template into another. To use the variable, we tell it which template group and template to embed. The variable is placed in the template that will be receiving the embedded template. Here's an example of the variable:

```
{embed="your_template_group/your_template"}
```

In the *Engine City Times* site, we're going to break out and embed the following parts of the template:

- Document header
- Masthead and navigation
- Category list
- Footer
- Search box and today's cartoon

We want to store all of our embedded templates in their own template group called *includes*. In the Template Manager, create a new template group, name it "includes," and save it. Now we can get started breaking up and embedding templates.

We'll start with the document header, which includes the DOCTYPE and everything between the header tags.

We want to take this chunk of code:

```
MakingthePages/template-home-ee.html
```

```
<!DOCTYPE html PUBLIC "-//W3C//DTD XHTML 1.0 Transitional//EN"
"http://www.w3.org/TR/xhtml1/DTD/xhtml1-transitional.dtd">

<html xmlns="http://www.w3.org/1999/xhtml"
xml:lang="en" lang="en">
<head>
 <meta http-equiv="Content-Type"
 content="text/html; charset=utf-8"/>

 <title>Engine City Times</title>
 <link rel="stylesheet" href="{stylesheet=site/site_css}"
 type="text/css" media="screen" />
</head>
```

and remove it from the index template and then replace it with an embed variable.

First, create a new template in the includes template group called "document_header." Remove the code from the index template, and place it in the newly created template.

Of course, now we have a gaping hole in the index template where the code was. In that space, place the embed variable, and point it at the includes template group and the document_header template. The variable should be placed at the very top of the template (in place of the content you removed) and should look like this:

```
{embed="includes/document_header"}
```

Save the index template, and reload the page. The home page should render just as it did before. You can use your browser's View Source command to check that the HTML is being embedded properly.

On Your Own

Now that you know how to do it, go ahead and create new templates for each template part listed earlier, and then embed those templates in the website index template. Do one at a time, and check after each one that the page renders properly.

After you're done, the top portion of the index template (with the top stories) should look like this:

```
MakingthePages/template-home-embeds-one.html
{embed="includes/document_header"}
<body class="home">
  <div id="layoutWrapper">
    {embed="includes/masthead"}
    <div id="content">
      <div id="top-stories">
        <h3>Top Stories</h3>
        <div id="lead-article">
          {exp:channel:entries channel="news_articles"
           limit="1" disable="pagination" status="Featured Top Story"}
          <img src="img/news-article-image.png" alt="" />
          <h4>{title}</h4>
          <h5><span class="by">By </span> {author}</h5>
          {article_excerpt}
          <p>
            <a href="{title_permalink="news_articles/view"}"
             class="read_story">Read Story</a>
          {/exp:channel:entries}
      </div><!-- END #lead-article -->

        <div id="sec-story-left">
          {exp:channel:entries channel="news_articles"
           disable="pagination" limit="2" status="Top Story"}
            <h4>{title}</h4>
            <h5><span class="by">By </span> {author}</h5>
            {article_excerpt}
            <p><a href="{title_permalink="news_articles/view"}"
                class="read_story">Read Story</a></p>
          {/exp:channel:entries}
        </div><!-- END #sec-story-left -->

        <div id="sec-story-right">
          {exp:channel:entries channel="news_articles"
           disable="pagination" limit="1" status="Top Story" offset="2"}
            <h4>{title}</h4>
            <h5><span class="by">By </span> {author}</h5>
            {article_excerpt}
            <p><a href="{title_permalink="news_articles/view"}"
                class="read_story">Read Story</a></p>
          {/exp:channel:entries}
        </div> <!-- END sec-story-right -->
        <div style="clear:both"></div>
      </div><!-- END #top-stories -->
```

The bottom portion of the template, which includes the sidebar, should be coded similar to the code at the top of the next page.

`MakingthePages/template-home-embeds-two.html`

```
<div id="to-editor">
  <h3>To the Editor</h3>
  <p class="subhead">Every day we publish some of
        your emails, letters and comments.</p>
   {exp:channel:entries channel="letters_to_editor" limit="3"}
     <div id="{switch="lcol|mcol|rcol"}">
       <h4>{title}</h4>
       <h5><span class="by">From</span> {author_name}</h5>
       {letter_copy}
     </div>
   {/exp:channel:entries}

   <p class="subhead">To submit your letter or comment,
        you can use our <a href="#">comment form</a> or
        email <a href="#">editor@enginecitytimes.com</a>.
        Letters may be edited for content, clarity and space
        constraints.</p>
</div>
<div style="clear:both;"></div><!-- END clear -->

</div><!-- END #content -->
<div id="topic-nav">
  {embed="includes/category_list"}
      {embed="includes/search_and_cartoon"}
    </div><!-- END #topic-nav -->

<div style="clear:left;"><br /></div><!-- END clear -->

{embed="includes/footer"}
```

5.4 Building Out the Article Template

On the home page, we linked every news article excerpt to a complete version using an anchor link that looked like this:

```
<a href="{title_permalink="news_articles/view"}"
class="read_story">Read Story</a>
```

Up to this point, the link that the ExpressionEngine code builds isn't functional because the "view" template we call doesn't exist yet. Let's create it now.

In the Template Manager, create a new blank template named "view" in the news_articles template group. In the directory of templates you downloaded, find the file template-article.html. Copy its entire contents into the new view template, and save it by clicking Update.

Adding the Embedded Templates

Before we get started lighting up the content areas of the view template, we want to first add the embedded templates we created in the previous section. Start with the document header, and embed the templates (we don't create any new ones because we can just reuse what's there!) one by one.

Once we've completed that, we click one of the Read Story links on the front page of the site, and it will lead to the view template we just created. Since we have not yet added ExpressionEngine tags to display content, we'll just see the static content from the template.

Lighting Up the Article Page

For this template, we'll use a similar process that we used to light up the home page except that we have different content. The article view page has the entire article copy, including the title and author. The article page also has reader discussion, which includes all recent reader comments, plus a form that readers can use to submit new comments. Finally, at the bottom of the page there is a section that contains three related articles. Let's start with the article content.

Article Content

To light up the article content, we'll use the same Channel Entries tag pair that we used for the home page, except this time we'll pull in the entire article copy instead of the excerpt using the {article_body} entry variable, which pulls the content from the custom field we created.

We want to use slightly different parameter settings for this template. The channel parameter will remain the same, but the status and limit parameters will need to be adjusted. Let's see how the final chunk of code should look, and then we'll discuss why it needs to be this way.

MakingthePages/template-article-ee.html

```
{exp:channel:entries channel="news_articles"
status="open|Featured Top Story|Top Story"
limit="1"}
<img src="/img/news-article-image.png"
alt="News Article Image" />
<h4>{title}</h4>
<h5><span class="by">By</span> {author}</h5>
{article_body}
{/exp:channel:entries}
```

The status parameter has the value of all possible statuses that would allow an article to appear on the site. Since this article view template is used by ExpressionEngine to display every article, we have to ensure it can do just that! By including every possible status, we can be sure every article will display properly, whether it's a top story, featured top story, or just a regular news article. Of course, we don't include the "closed" status because articles with that status have not received editorial approval to be published on the site. To include more than one value in a parameter, you separate it using what's called a *pipe* (|) character.

The limit parameter is also included but with a value of 1. Since the article view will only ever be used to display a single article, you would think we don't need to specify a limit. The template would function without it, but by setting the limit to 1, we eliminate the possibility of someone seeing every single article in the database listed if they visit the site using an incorrect article URL. Try it for yourself. Change the last segment of the URL of an article page, and watch as ExpressionEngine loads in every article in the database. Right now it's only a few, so it's nothing more than a ugly page. But down the road when the *Engine City Times* site has thousands of articles, ExpressionEngine will attempt to load them all, and that could possibly negatively affect the performance of the web server. So, to be safe, always set a limit of 1 on individual article pages.

If you haven't already, add or adjust the article code in the view template so it looks the snippet listed earlier. Save the template, and reload the page to see the individual article.

Article Comments

With the article content displayed, we can now turn our attention to the reader comments and comment submission form that accompanies every news article on the site. The ability to comment on every news article was enabled when we created the news_articles channel and set its preferences in Chapter 4, *Creating and Configuring the Site*, on page 43.

Let's first focus on the comment submission form. We'll get it up and running first, add a few comments, and then add the code to display those comments. We don't need to make many changes to the comment form to get it working with ExpressionEngine. The first thing we want to do is replace the opening and closing form tags with these special ExpressionEngine Comment Form tags:

```
{exp:comment:form}
...
{/exp:comment:form}
```

We can keep the form elements for name, email, and comment text, but we just need to add some variables to the *value* parameters, so our final form looks like this:

`MakingthePages/template-article-ee.html`

```
        {exp:comment:form channel="news_articles"}
        <p><label for="name">Name</label><br />
        <input type="text" name="name"
value="{name}" id="name" size="37" /></p>
        <p><label for="email">Email Address</label><br />
        <input type="text" name="email" value="{email}"
id="email" size="37" /></p>
        <p><label for="comment">Comment</label><br />
        <textarea name="comment" rows="8" cols="35"
id="comment">{comment}</textarea></p>
        <p><input type="submit" name="submit"
value="Submit" /></p>
        {/exp:comment:form}
```

Make the changes so your template looks like the previous code, and then save the template. Reload the article view in the browser, and the form should look the same. Go ahead and fill it out with a test comment, and click Submit. ExpressionEngine will save the comment and then return you to the article page. Add at least three comments to the news article.[3] Once you've done that, we'll need to make our newly added comment display under the article.

Above the comment form are the three sample comments. If we look at the template, we'll see that each comment is marked up as a definition list, which is contained in a div. There are three parts to every comment: comment author name, comment date, and comment body. Also notice that every other comment has a gray background. We'll need to account for that when adding the ExpressionEngine code to light up the comments.

For the comment submission form, we used the {exp:comment:form} tag pair. For displaying the entries, we'll use a corresponding tag pair:

```
{exp:comment:entries}
...
{/exp:comment:entries}
```

We want to wrap this tag pair around the "comment-content" div and then replace the comment author's name with the {name} variable, the

---

3. Unless you log out from the Control Panel, ExpressionEngine will create every comment with you as the user, no matter what you enter into the Name and Email fields.

comment date with {comment_date format="%F %d, %Y"}, and the comment text with the {comment} variable.

To make the background color of the comment alternate, we need to use the {switch} variable again. The classes of odd and even get applied to the div that surrounds each comment. We just need to replace the second class (leave the class comment-content in place) with the {switch} variable so it alternates between "even" and "odd."

The final chunk of code for displaying comments should look like this:

MakingthePages/template-article-ee.html

```
{exp:comment:entries channel="news_articles"}
<div class="comment-content {switch="odd|even"}">
  <dl>
    <dt><span class="posted-by">
          Posted by</span> {name}
    <span class="comment-date">
    {comment_date format="%F %d, %Y"}
    </span></dt>
    <dd>{comment}</dd>
  </dl>
</div>
{/exp:comment:entries}
```

Save these changes to your article view template, and then reload the page to see your comments listed. If you have at least two comments, the alternating background color should look like Figure 5.5, on the next page.

Displaying Related Articles

The final part of the article view template that needs to be integrated into ExpressionEngine is the Related Articles section at the bottom of the page. You should recognize the layout of this section, because it's exactly the same as the To the Editor section on the front page of the site. Look at the HTML for this section, and it should definitely look familiar. There are three columns, each with their own id: lcol, mcol, and rcol.

Before we add the ExpressionEngine code to make the related articles display, let's briefly discuss how we're going to tell ExpressionEngine to show articles that are somehow related to the one being viewed. There are complex ways to do this—based on tags and relationships between entries—but we'll keep it simple for this site and define related articles as those that belong to the same category as the article being

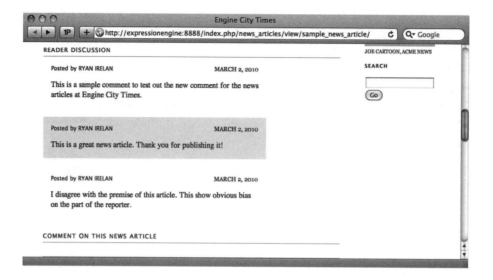

Figure 5.5: Displaying comments with alternating backgrounds using the SWITCH parameter

shown. Luckily for us, ExpressionEngine has a parameter we can set in a Channel Entries tag pair to make this happen almost automatically: related_categories_mode="yes". Placed in the Channel Entries tag pair, it would look like this:

```
{exp:channel:entries channel="news_articles"
related_categories_mode="yes" custom_fields="yes"}
...
{/exp:channel:entries}
```

Whenever we use related categories, we have to explicitly enable custom fields, which in most other situations are on by default. If we don't turn that on, the custom fields we created in the previous chapter won't show when we view the page in the browser. The folks who make ExpressionEngine turned off custom fields when using related categories as a way to reduce the load on the database.

The other parameters we need to include in the Channel Entries tag pair are limit="3" and status="Open|Top Story|Featured Top Story". Let's add these parameters to the previous code, and wrap the Channel Entries tag pair around the div that displays the related articles.

To make sure we get the nice three-column layout, we have to once again use the {switch} variable to rotate between ids for the divs that create the columns.

Finally, we need to plug in the entry variables so the content displays. We'll use {title}, {author}, and {article_excerpt} for the article content and {title_permalink="news_articles/view"} to link up the "Read Story" text to the individual article view page. The final chunk of code should look like this:

MakingthePages/template-article-ee.html

```
    <h3>Related Articles</h3>
        {exp:channel:entries channel="news_articles"
related_categories_mode="yes" disable="pagination"
limit="3" status="open|Top Story|Featured Top Story"
custom_fields="yes" dynamic="no"}
    <div id="{switch="lcol|mcol|rcol"}">
        <h4>{title}</h4>
        <h5><span class="by">By</span> {author}</h5>
        {article_excerpt}
        <p><a href="{title_permalink="news_articles/view"}"
class="read_story">Read Story</a></p>
    </div>
        {/exp:channel:entries}
```

Make these changes in your template, save it, and then load the article view in a browser. At the bottom you should see three articles, similar to Figure 5.6, on the following page. Clicking the Read Story link should bring you to the article page for another news story where there also will be related articles at the bottom of the page.

With two of the three templates that power the *Engine City Times* website complete, the site is slowly coming to life with dynamic content. We have only one template left to light up: the category template.

5.5 Lighting Up the Category Template

The final template to build for this phase of the site is the one that displays the category page for articles. If a user clicks World—listed under the News category—a page will display that has all the news articles filed under the World category.

In the template directory you downloaded, open template-category.html in your browser to see how the category page will look. At the top of the page there is the category name, below that three articles with excerpts,

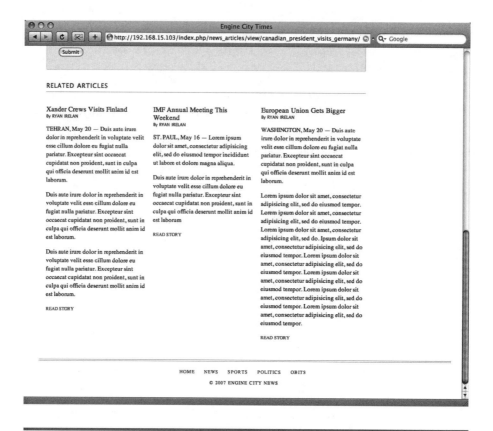

Figure 5.6: DYNAMICALLY DISPLAYING RELATED ARTICLES

and below that a listing of article titles, all linked to the full version of each. To the right is a placeholder for a cartoon image.

Let's create a new template in the news_articles template group called "page." Copy and paste the static HTML into the newly created template, and save it. Using the examples from earlier in the chapter, add embedded templates where needed so we're reusing markup and ExpressionEngine code that is shared among the site templates.

Displaying the Category Name

At the top of the page is the name of the category that is being viewed. Since this template is being used for every category on the site, we can't hard-code it with a category name. We have to set it up so it dynamically displays the category name. To do this, we'll use the ExpressionEngine tag pair {exp:channel:category_heading}. The sole purpose of this tag pair is to do exactly what we're using it for: display the name of the currently viewed category.

We just have to add the channel parameter, giving it a value of news_ articles, and wrap the tag pair around the h3 that displays the category name. The code in your template should look like this:

`MakingthePages/template-category-ee.html`

```
{exp:channel:category_heading channel="news_articles"}
<h3>{category_name}</h3>
{/exp:channel:category_heading}
```

After making these changes, save the template, and click one of the category names from the list on the far right to test the template. You should see the static category template, but the category name at the top of the page should change according to the category you clicked. With that set, we can get started displaying the category content.

Displaying the Category Content

We have two content areas to display in this template: the three latest articles and a simple list of titles of any other articles filed under this category. Since we've done this together a couple of times already, I'm going to hand this part off to you to do on your own. Everything that is required we've already done together, but here are some hints:

- *Latest Three Articles*: Use the {switch} parameter for the column ids, and don't forget to link up the "Read Story" text.
- *List of Article Titles*: This is a simple unordered list of titles and links. Let's limit this to the latest twenty articles (although only one will show because our site is not yet populated with content). Just like with the other page elements, you need only one li element, and ExpressionEngine will loop through and create one for each article it finds.

Good luck!

Checking Your Work

I'm sure you did a bang-up job on the category template, but just in case you had some problems or want to check your work against my templates, the next page shows how your category template should look.

```
MakingthePages/template-category-ee.html
```

```
{embed="includes/document_header"}
<body class="home">
  <div id="layoutWrapper">
  {embed="includes/masthead"}
  <div id="content">
    <div id="category-featured">
    {exp:channel:category_heading channel="news_articles"}
    <h3>{category_name}</h3>
    {/exp:channel:category_heading}
    {exp:channel:entries channel="news_articles"
disable="pagination" limit="3"
status="open|Top Story|Featured Top Story"}
      <div id="{switch="lcol|mcol|rcol"}">
        <h4>{title}</h4>
        <h5><span class="by">By</span> {author}</h5>
        {article_excerpt}
        <p><a href="{title_permalink="news_articles/view"}"
          class="read_story">Read Story</a></p>
      </div>
      {/exp:channel:entries}
    </div><!-- END #category-featured -->
    <div style="clear:both;"></div><!-- END clear -->
    <div id="category-articles">
      <ul>
        {exp:channel:entries channel="news_articles"
        disable="custom_fields" limit="20"
        status="open|Top Story|Featured Top Story" offset="3"}
        <li><a href="{title_permalink="news_articles/view"}">
            {title}</a></li>
        {/exp:channel:entries}
      </ul>
    </div>
  </div><!-- END #content -->
  <div id="topic-nav">
  {embed="includes/category_list"}
  {embed="includes/search_and_cartoon"}
  </div><!-- END #topic-nav -->
  <div style="clear:left;"><br /></div><!-- END clear -->
{embed="includes/footer"}
```

5.6 What We Learned

In this chapter, we built out almost every template for the website and added ExpressionEngine code to display content dynamically. Along the way, we learned about parameters that control how ExpressionEngine displays content, generated a complete list of all article categories, and broke up the template code into "embeddable" templates, which allow us to reuse code throughout the site's templates.

In the next chapter, we'll add some spit and polish to the *Engine City Times* website by adding an RSS feed, search functionality, and navigation. The site is quickly coming together!

Chapter 6

Adding the Final Touches

The *Engine City Times* website is almost complete. Left on our list of to-dos is to add an RSS feed, light up the search box, create a search results page, add a static About page, and light up the navigation. After all of that, you'll be ready to finalize the site by adding the Obituaries section on your own.

Now that the site is almost completely built, we'll get into the finer details, and we'll continue adding new ExpressionEngine site-building skills to our tool belt.

6.1 Adding a Static Page

Up to this point the only type of content we have dealt with was collections—a set of news articles and letters to the editor. But we can also create single pages in ExpressionEngine. Pages are static content—assigned to a URI—that we can create and edit through the Control Panel. This functionality is available through the Pages module, which ships with all versions of ExpressionEngine. To use the module, we have to first install and configure it.

Installing the Pages Module

To install the module, click the Add-Ons button, and then select Modules. Find Pages in the list of modules. To the far right of the Pages line, click Install. If the install worked, you should now see the word "Pages" hyperlinked. But before we access the Pages module, we first need to create a site channel to store the page's content, custom fields to enter the page content, and a template to display the page on the website.

Why do we have to create a site channel for the Pages module? ExpressionEngine stores the pages as entries in a channel but displays them as individual pages where you can explicitly set the URI. Because of this, we need to create a site channel to hold our pages. Up to this point, the *Engine City Times* site has three channels: Letters to the Editor, News Articles, and Obituaries. Let's create a new channel and name it "Static Content." We want to configure it similarly to Letters to the Editor—with pagination disabled.

Next, we need to create a field group for the page's content. Create a new one with a field for the page copy (call it page_copy and make it a textarea). Assign that field group to the "Static Content" section that we created.

We also need to create a new template that we'll use to display the pages. We can use the same template for every static page we create. We'll call the template static and create it in the site template group. Paste in the code from the template-static.html file that you downloaded from the book website, and save the template. Be sure to replace the code we extracted into embedded templates. Use an existing template as a guide, and refer to Chapter 5, *Making the Pages*, on page 67 if you need a refresher on how we set up the templates for the *Engine City Times* website.

Now we need to light up the static template using a Channel Entries tag pair that calls the static_content channel. Wrap the content in a Channel Entries tag pair, and replace the sample content with the necessary tag variables. Your template should look like this:

```
AddingtheFinalTouches/staticTemplate.html
```

```
{embed="includes/document_header"}
<body class="home">
 <div id="layoutWrapper">
 {embed="includes/masthead"}
 <div id="content">
  <div id="article">
  {exp:channel:entries channel="static_content"
   disable="pagination" limit="1"}
  <h4>{title}</h4>
  {page_copy}
  {/exp:channel:entries}
  </div>
 </div><!-- END #content -->
 <div id="topic-nav">
 {embed="includes/category_list"}
 {embed="includes/search_and_cartoon"}
 </div><!-- END #topic-nav -->
```

> ### Making It Easier to Access the Pages Module
>
> By default, the Pages module is buried in the list of modules in the Modules section of the Control Panel. We want to make Pages accessible via a button at the top of the Control Panel. To do this, navigate to the Pages module, and then click the red "+ Add" text to the right of the row of buttons. This will automatically create a Pages button for you. Now, it's much easier for us and the *Engine City Times* editors to manage and create new pages.

```
<div style="clear:both;"></div><!-- END clear -->
{embed="includes/footer"}
</div><!-- END #layoutWrapper -->
</body>
</html>
```

Navigate to the Pages module, and you should see a blank page with the text "No Pages Currently Exist." Before we can get started creating static pages, we need to first configure the module using the Module Configuration button at the top right. Here we need to set the three configuration options for the module.

For a nicer look, we'd like to have the display of URIs on the module home page be nested, so set that option using the drop-down menu. All of our static pages will be saved into the newly created Static Content channel in ExpressionEngine, so we want to make that the default channel. Finally, we'll set the default template for the Static Content channel to site/static. We can leave the others alone for now, because we won't be setting up those sections to publish static pages. Click Update to save the changes. This will bring you back to the main Pages screen, and now we can create our first page!

Creating the About Page

We're going to create an About page for the newspaper. It will be a simple page with a title and a couple of paragraphs of content that will describe the newspaper and its history. The client will fill in the final content, so we'll just add some dummy content in the interim.

Click the gray Create New Page button to get to the entry form. To see the Pages-specific fields, click the small Pages tab at the top of the form.

The Pages module allows you to set exactly what you want the URI of the page to be. For the About page, we want to set the URI to /about/. The template can stay how it is because it just uses the default we set earlier when we configured the Pages module.

Give the page a title of "About" and then add some sample content to the Page Copy field. When you're done, save the page using the Submit button. You should now be able to view the page in the browser by going to the site URL for the page, which should be something like this: http://yourdomain.com/index.php/about/.

Now that the Pages module is set up, we can create as many pages as we want. In fact, I think you should do just that.

On Your Own

As a bit of homework, create a new page in the *Engine City Times* website that will hold contact information. There won't be a contact form, but just an address and phone number.

After you're done making the page, add both it and the About page we created earlier to the navigation in the footer. You can edit it using the footer template, located in the includes template group.

While you're creating pages, try nesting them like this: /about/me or /about/you/. Then see how ExpressionEngine displays them nested on the Pages module overview page. Make as many pages as you need to get comfortable with how they work and how ExpressionEngine handles the URIs you create.

6.2 Lighting Up the Navigation

We haven't touched the main navigation at all since creating the templates for the *Engine City Times* website. You may have wondered whether we'd ever get those working. Well, now is the time.

Linking the Navigation Items

The first step in lighting up the navigation is to link the navigation items to the proper URIs. To do this, open the masthead template in the includes template group.

Edit the template so the navigation links look like this:

`AddingtheFinalTouches/masthead_one.html`

```
<ul>
 <li><a href="/">Home</a></li>
 <li><a href="/index.php/news_articles/page/
 category/news">News</a></li>
 <li><a href="/index.php/news_articles/page/
 category/sports">Sports</a></li>
 <li><a href="/index.php/news_articles/page/
 category/politics">Politics</a></li>
 <li><a href="">Obits</a></li>
</ul>
```

Notice that we're leaving the Obituaries item unlinked. Later in the chapter you'll have some homework and can take care of that then. Save the template, load the website in your browser, and test the navigation links.

The problem we have now is that we want to change how each item in the navigation displays when its page or section is displayed. For example, when the News page is displayed, the News navigation item should be highlighted with the dark gray background color that is currently being used for Home. How do we solve this? It's all very easy with the power of ExpressionEngine conditionals.

Creating a Dynamic Navigation with ExpressionEngine Conditionals

In ExpressionEngine, *conditionals* allow you to control what information is displayed based on different decisions. There are two types of conditionals in ExpressionEngine—conditional global variables and channel entries conditional variables. The latter are only used inside the Channel Entries tag pair and are specific to content. The other conditionals you can use almost anywhere.

If you're familiar with any programming languages, you'll quickly catch on to the syntax of ExpressionEngine conditionals. Here's a simple example:

```
{if logged_in}
       You are logged in.
{/if}
```

This simple conditional checks whether the visitor is logged in to ExpressionEngine. If they are, the "You are logged in" message appears. If not, the message does not show.

There is also the option to do something if the condition is not met. Here's an example:

```
{if logged_in}
    You are logged in.
{if:else}
        Please log in.
{/if}
```

The {if:else} variable gives you finer control by telling ExpressionEngine what to do in the event that the first conditional is not met. In this example, ExpressionEngine will display the "You are logged in" text if the user is logged in. If not, the "Please log in" text will display.

Taking it a step further, let's use something called the *URL segment* to check which page of the site we're on and then display code in the template based on whether that condition is met.

URL Segments

ExpressionEngine breaks every URL it generates into segments, starting after the index.php. The first segment is segment_1, the second is segment_2, the third is segment_3, and so on. Segments are commonly used to control what information is presented on a page depending on which page you're on. Here's an example of that:

```
{if segment_1 == "news_articles"}
You are reading news articles.
{/if}
```

This conditional checks the first segment of the URL, and if it is equivalent to "news_articles," the text will show. You can probably see where we're going with this. Using conditionals, we can make our navigation dynamic so it always knows the page we're on.

Making Smart Navigation

Our goal is to make the navigation highlight the item that is currently displayed. If we're on the Politics page, the Politics navigation item should be highlighted. We can make this happen with a combination of URL segments and conditionals that we just learned about.

To make it happen, we want to check for the current page, and if it matches the one that belongs to the navigation item, we'll add a class to the anchor link so the CSS alters the display. To see how it will look, view the site and look at the Home item in the navigation. In the template, that item is marked up like this:

```
<li><a class="current" href="/">Home</a></li>
```

To highlight the navigation item, we just add a class="current". What we need to do now is use a conditional to check whether we're on a certain URL segment. Let's jump into the code that'll make it work:

`AddingtheFinalTouches/masthead.html`

```
<li><a {if segment_1 == ""}class="current"
{/if} href="/">Home</a></li>
```

This uses a simple conditional that checks whether segment_1 is empty (which means we're on the home page of the site), and if it is, we display class="current". We will do the same for the other links but with a slight adjustment. Instead of checking for the first segment, we need to check for the fourth, where the category name is listed. Additionally, instead of using empty quotes, we'll check that the category name in the fourth segment matches the name of the navigation items. Here's the final code for our main navigation:

`AddingtheFinalTouches/masthead.html`

```
<ul>
 <li><a {if segment_1 == ""}class="current"
 {/if} href="/">Home</a></li>
 <li><a {if segment_4 == "news"}class="current"
 {/if}href="/index.php/news_articles
 /page/category/news">News</a></li>
 <li><a {if segment_4 == "sports"}class="current"
 {/if}href="/index.php/news_articles
 /page/category/sports">Sports</a></li>
 <li><a {if segment_4 == "politics"}class="current"
 {/if}href="/index.php/news_articles
 /page/category/politics">Politics</a></li>
 <li><a href="">Obits</a></li>
</ul>
```

Add this code to your masthead template, and save the changes. Load the front page of the *Engine City Times* in your website, and test the navigation. As you click each one, the proper page should display, and the navigation item is highlighted. The only one that won't work is Obits because we haven't yet created that section of the site. That will be your homework at the end of this chapter.

6.3 Cleaning Up Using Conditionals

We just learned the basics about ExpressionEngine conditionals and used them to alter how our navigation displays. Let's also use them to clean up how some of our content displays on the site.

There are two scenarios on the *Engine City Times* website where content can be cleaned up using conditionals. The first is when there are no comments on an article. If you navigate to an article on the site that doesn't have comments, you'll see that the header "Reader Discussion" is immediately followed by "Comment on this News Article." This looks awkward. If there aren't any comments, we want to display a short message that encourages the reader to comment; it should be something like "Be the first to comment, using the form below!"

In the previous section, I briefly mentioned the channel entries conditional variables. This is a special set of conditional variables that you can use only inside a Channel Entries tag pair. There are also some special variables in the Comment Entries tag pair, and we'll use one to display our message if an article has no comments.

The conditional variable we'll use is called if no_results, and if it evaluates to true, it displays whatever is between the tag pair. Here's how it would work for our implementation:

```
{if no_results}
<p>
        Be the first to comment, using the form below!
 </p>
{/if}
```

We place this in between the Comment Entries tag pair like so:

`AddingtheFinalTouches/comments-conditional.html`

```
{exp:comment:entries channel="news_articles"}

 {if no_results}
  <p>Be the first to comment, using the form below!</p>
 {/if}

<div class="comment-content {switch="odd|even"}">
 <dl>
  <dt><span class="posted-by">Posted by</span> {name}
        <span class="comment-date">
                {comment_date format="%F %d, %Y"}
                </span></dt>
   <dd>{comment}</dd>
 </dl>
</div>

{/exp:comment:entries}
```

Add the conditional code to the view template in the news_articles template group. Save the template, and load an article that has no comments. The message to the reader should now appear. If we add a comment, the message will go away.

The second scenario is when an article has no related articles. Once the newspaper populates the site with content, this may be a fringe case, but it could still happen, and we should account for it. Rather than show a "Related Articles" header with nothing below it, let's show a short message stating that there are no related entries for this article.

To achieve this, we'll use the channel entries version of if no_results. Similar to comments, this conditional is used to display content if for some reason the Channel Entries tag pair returns no entries.

```
{if no_results}
<p>There are no related articles.</p>
{/if}
```

Add this code into the view template, specifically in the Channel Entries tag pair for the Related Articles section. Your code should look like this:

AddingtheFinalTouches/related-articles.html

```
<h3>Related Articles</h3>
 {exp:channel:entries channel="news_articles"
  related_categories_mode="yes"
  disable="pagination" limit="3"
  status="Open|Top Story|Featured Top Story"
  custom_fields="yes"}
 {if no_results}
  <p>There are no related articles.</p>
 {/if}
 <div id="{switch="lcol|mcol|rcol"}">
  <h4>{title}</h4>
  <h5><span class="by">By</span> {author}</h5>
  {article_excerpt}
  <p><a href="{title_permalink="news_articles/view"}"
       class="read_story">Read Story</a></p>
 </div>
 {/exp:channel:entries}
```

Save the template, and then create a new entry using a category to which you have not yet published an article. I'd suggest something under Sports. After creating the article, load it in the browser, and at the bottom you should see "the no related articles" message.

There are almost limitless uses of ExpressionEngine conditionals, but these two examples are some of the simplest and most common implementations. You'll find that ExpressionEngine conditionals come in handy for making websites more dynamic and responsive to where the user is on the website. By learning the basics of ExpressionEngine conditionals, you are now prepared to face many of the challenges presented while building websites with ExpressionEngine.

6.4 Creating an RSS Feed

The *Engine City Times* editors want to offer an alternative method for readers to get news articles, so they've opted to publish an RSS feed. It will be accessible at the top of every page on the site, just to the right of the main navigation.

Creating the feed is a three-step process: we create the RSS feed template in ExpressionEngine, edit the template to work with our site, and then validate the feed using a "feed validator" so we're sure it will work in most every RSS reader.

ExpressionEngine provides you with almost everything you need to get an RSS feed up and running. The first thing we want to do is create a template called feed in the site template group. We want to give it the template type of RSS Page and create an empty template. After you create it, you'll notice it shows up in the template list with a small feed icon next to it. If it doesn't, you may not have set the proper template type.

We won't have to create the code for the RSS template from scratch because EllisLab, the makers of ExpressionEngine, offer RSS templates on its site.[1] Copy the RSS 2.0 template, and paste the entire thing into the newly created feed template. At time of publication of this book, the feed template is still coded for a previous version of ExpressionEngine. You will need to convert all instances of "weblog" to "channel" to get this feed working properly. I've done this for you in the template included in the downloadable code available on the book website. Click Update to save the template.

Now that we have the default ExpressionEngine template, we need to customize it so it will work with our *Engine City Times* website. We will start at the top by setting the preload replace variable master_channel_name.

AddingtheFinalTouches/rss.html

```
{preload_replace:master_channel_name="news_articles"}
```

1. http://expressionengine.com/templates/source/category/feeds/

This variable is referenced throughout the template, so we only need to declare once that we want to create a feed of all news articles. Because we're pulling only from the news_articles channel, we need to edit the title tag so it has the name of the site.

```
<title>{exp:xml_encode}{channel_name}{/exp:xml_encode}</title>
```

If we leave it as is, the feed will show that the site name is "News Articles," which is the name of the channel we're displaying. We'll use the site_name variable, so the line looks like this:

`AddingtheFinalTouches/rss.html`

```
<title>{exp:xml_encode}{site_name}{/exp:xml_encode}</title>
```

Now when an RSS reader displays the feed, it will have the site's name.

The next line we need to change is the URL that ExpressionEngine uses to point to each article so the reader can click through and read the full article on the *Engine City Times* website. The link in the RSS feed is created in this line of template code:

```
<link>{title_permalink=site/index}</link>
```

The title permalink isn't set to how we have our news article template group and template named, so we need to adjust it like this:

`AddingtheFinalTouches/rss.html`

```
<link>{title_permalink="news_articles/view"}</link>
```

Now the link to each news article in the RSS feed will point the correct URL of the article.

The final change needed is to the variables used to display the content, which is located one line below the previous change. The default RSS template uses channel entry variables from the default field group. Since we customized ExpressionEngine, we need to tell it which content to show. The newspaper wants to show only the excerpt of the article, so the readers will have to click and visit the site to read the entire article.

We want to replace the two variables in the template with the article_excerpt variable, so the line looks like this:

`AddingtheFinalTouches/rss.html`

```
<description>{exp:xml_encode}
{article_excerpt}{/exp:xml_encode}</description>
```

Now the RSS feed will show the excerpt only. Save these changes to the template.

Now we want to validate the feed to check that it is valid and will display in most every RSS reader. To do this, we take the feed URL and submit it to the feed validator website.[2] Your feed URL will be your domain plus index.php/feed.[3] Submit your feed to the feed validator site to check that it is valid. If it is, your feed is all set.

Before we move on, let's go back into the masthead template and add the feed URL to the subscribe link. That part of your template should look similar to this:

AddingtheFinalTouches/rssLink.html

```
<a href="http://yourdomain.com/index.php/feed"> <p id="subscribe">
<img src="/img/feed-icon.png"
alt="feed icon" />Subscribe to the News</a></p>
```

Save the template, load the website front page, and test the subscribe link.

Let's review what we've done so far. Up to this point you should have a working RSS feed and dynamic navigation using ExpressionEngine conditionals. Now let's move forward and add some search functionality to our website.

6.5 Adding Search Functionality

On every page of the *Engine City Times* there is a small search box in the side column below the categories list. Currently, it does nothing, so we want to light it up so the readers of Engine City News website can search all of the news articles on the site.

When we set up the News Articles section, we set the option "Make available to search" to Yes. This tells ExpressionEngine that these fields should be used to return search results.

ExpressionEngine uses the Search module, which is provided with ExpressionEngine, to create the search functionality. It provides us with an easy way to create simple and advanced search forms and search results pages. The module comes preinstalled, so we don't have to do anything to get started.

---

2. http://feedvalidator.org
3. http://yourdomain.com/index.php/feed

Making a Simple Search Form

Creating a simple search form in ExpressionEngine is really as simple as the name implies. We use the Simple Search Form tag pair, which we wrap around a text input field and input button. Here's the search from the HTML code on our site:

`AddingtheFinalTouches/search-static.html`

```
<dt id="search-box">Search</dt>
<dd>
 <form action="template-article_submit"
       method="post" accept-charset="utf-8">
  <input type="text" name="search"
         value="" id="search"
         size="17" />
  <p><input type="submit" value="Go"></p>
 </form>
</dd>
```

To get this form working, we just need to replace the form tags with the ExpressionEngine Simple Search Form tags:

`AddingtheFinalTouches/search-ee.html`

```
<dt id="search-box">Search</dt>
<dd>
{exp:search:simple_form channel="news_articles"}
<input type="text" name="keywords" value=""
       id="search" size="17" />
<input type="submit" value="Go">
{/exp:search:simple_form}
</dd>
```

The Simple Search Form tag pair takes several parameters, including the channel parameter and the search_in parameter. Since we want to allow readers to search only news articles, I made news_articles the value of the channel parameter. It also takes a search_in parameter to tell ExpressionEngine where to search in the entries. By default ExpressionEngine searches only the titles. We set the values of the search_in parameter to "everywhere" to tell ExpressionEngine to search inside all available fields (unless we explicitly marked the field as not searchable when we configured our custom fields).

The search will work, but ExpressionEngine won't know which template to use to display the results. We need to add the parameter result_page that will tell ExpressionEngine which template to render to display the results.

AddingtheFinalTouches/search-ee-2.html

```
<dt id="search-box">Search</dt>
<dd>
{exp:search:simple_form channel="news_articles"
 search_in="everywhere" result_page="site/search"}
<input type="text" name="keywords" value=""
       id="search" size="17" />
<input type="submit" value="Go">
{/exp:search:simple_form}
</dd>
```

We are now telling ExpressionEngine to display the search template, which will be located in the site template group. We'll create the template in the next section.

Add this updated form code to the cartoon_and_search template we created in the previous chapter, and save it.

Creating the Search Results Template

Create an empty template named "search" in the site template group, and paste in the code from template-search-results.html from the directory of templates you downloaded from the book website. Be sure to edit the template so it uses the same embedded templates (from the includes template group) that the rest of the templates use (if you've forgotten how to do this, refer to Chapter 5, *Making the Pages*, on page 67). After you've done that, save the template.

Load the template in the browser to get an idea of what it will look like. Using a definition list, the template lists the title and article excerpt for each search result. Each title is linked to the article view page.

Back in the Control Panel, edit the template, and light it up using the Search Results tag pair that ExpressionEngine provides.

```
{exp:search:search_results}
  ...
{/exp:search:search_results}
```

We will start by wrapping our search results with the tag pair. The next step is to add the variables to display the content. We use the same variables we used for displaying the new articles in other parts of the site.

AddingtheFinalTouches/search-ee-results.html

```
<h4>Search Results</h4>
<dl id="search_results">
{exp:search:search_results}
```

```
<dt><a href="{title_permalink="news_articles/view"}">
{title}</a></dt>
<dd>{article_excerpt}</dd>
{/exp:search:search_results}
</dl>
```

I removed all the static content from the results listing and replaced it with the entry variables. We're going to display the article title and excerpt and, using the title_permalink variable, link the title to the article view page. Make these changes to your template, and save it. Using a keyword from one of your articles, test the search to see how the results look. The search results will be limited until the *Engine City Times* staff begins populating the site with content.

6.6 On Your Own

Most of the major functionality of the site is now complete. Although there are some leftover items that we'll address throughout the remainder of the book, there is one gaping hole left: the Obituaries section. I need your help with this, and it will give you the opportunity to use all of the information and skills acquired over the previous three chapters to complete this task.

We've already created the Obituaries section and template group. You need to create the necessary templates and light them up with ExpressionEngine tags. There aren't premade templates for you to use. My suggestion would be to use the news category template but remove the large cartoon image.

Good luck!

6.7 What We Learned

With the *Engine City Times* website now complete in basic functionality, we've successfully built our first ExpressionEngine site from installation to implementation. Throughout this part of the book we learned all of the basic skills needed to begin building any website on ExpressionEngine. It's true that every site will require a different setup and present different challenges. However, since we've already seen a site through from inception to end, we can meet the challenge of building a website with ExpressionEngine.

Moving forward, we will build on the techniques presented up to this point, further refining them and adding complexity that will prepare us for even the most challenging of websites. In the next section of the book, we get more advanced. The tasks are set up so we can build on the *Engine City Times* website and the skills learned up to this point. We'll learn about sharing data between templates with embed variables, working with templates as files instead of inside the Control Panel and allowing site visitors to submit their own content right into the ExpressionEngine database.

Because we're so well-prepared with the basic ExpressionEngine skills, from here on out we'll quickly increase our ExpressionEngine knowledge and begin to anticipate problems and quickly devise their solutions. This is where the real joy of building websites with ExpressionEngine is born.

Part III

Digging In

Chapter 7

Creating Relationships
Between Entries

Creating relationships between entries is essential in keeping your website content as simple and organized as possible. It prevents you from having to store the same data in multiple places.

Let's say you're building an About page for a business website that lists employees and their respective departments. You could store the department name in a field in a channel entry for each employee. But what happens if that department name changes? You would have to go through each and every employee entry and change the name.

You can prevent this scenario by creating another channel called "departments," creating an entry for each department, and then relating an employee to a department. Now, if the department name changes, you only have to edit in one place: the entry for that department. All of the employees in that department will then display the new name.

Relating entries lets you take many different channel entries and organize them under a common umbrella. That is exactly what we'll be doing for our sample website.

With the basic *Engine City Times* website done, the editors at the newspaper have asked for some additional functionality. They want to be able to organize some articles on their website by the print edition of the newspaper in which they appeared.

Here's what we need to accomplish:

- Give editors the ability to create new print editions for each day

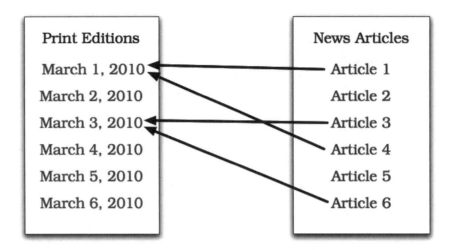

Figure 7.1: IN THESE ENTRY RELATIONSHIPS, THE PRINT EDITIONS ARE THE PARENTS, AND THE NEWS ARTICLES ARE THE CHILDREN.

- Display a page for each print edition and its articles

- Show a list of recent print editions on the sidebar of the *Engine City Times* website

Using the related entries functionality in ExpressionEngine, we will implement this request from the newspaper. But first let's cover the basics about related entries and how they work.

7.1 Building Entry Relationships

Related entries allow us to create a relationship between one entry and one or more others. In our case, we'll create a relationship between an entry in the Print Edition channel (we need to create this channel) and some News Articles channel entries. In our templates, we will use special related entry tags to retrieve and display the related entries.

In Figure 7.1, we can see how we'll use related entries.

The print editions are the parents, and the news articles are the children. One or more news articles can be related to a print edition. In Figure 7.1, both Article 1 and Article 4 are related to the March 1,

2010, print edition. Similarly, both Article 3 and Article 6 are related to the March 3, 2010, print edition.

There are two ways to display related entries in ExpressionEngine: straight related entries and reverse related entries. Let's look at them both.

Related Entries

Straight related entries are used to display information about the parent when viewing one of its children. So, if we were viewing a news article, we could display the print edition to which that news article belongs. To do this, we use the Related Entries tag pair:

```
{related_entries id="print_edition"}
 <p><em>Published in print on {title}</em>.</p>
{/related_entries}
```

The Related Entries tag pair has a required parameter of id whose value should be the custom field that contains the relationship (we'll create this field later in Section 7.2, *Setting Up Related Entries*, on the next page). Because this code must live in the Channel Entries tag pair, we can use any custom fields available in the parent channel. In the code example, we're just displaying the related entry's title.

Reverse Related Entries

To display a print edition and all of its children, we need to use the Reverse Related Entries tag pair. Why reverse? Because unlike in the previous code sample, we are displaying the parent plus the children. To get a list of news articles that are related to the print edition, we'll need to get the reverse relationship. We'll go over the code in more detail in Section 7.3, *Writing Related Entries Template Code*, on page 118, but here is the tag pair for reverse related entries:

```
{reverse_related_entries sort="desc"}
...
{/reverse_related_entries}
```

Just like the Related Entries tag pair, the Reverse Related Entries tag pair has to live in the Channel Entries tag pair. This will output all of the child entries of the parent entry.

Let's get started building the print editions for the *Engine City Times*.

7.2 Setting Up Related Entries

To create relationships between entries, we need to have two separate channels in place and some entries available in each. It is required to have all of the content channels set up first before creating any relationships.

Since the *Engine City Times* would like to be able to view a page for each print edition, we need to first set up the new channel to hold the print edition entries.

Navigate to the Channel Management section of the Control Panel. Create a new channel with a full channel name of "Print Editions" and a channel name of "print_editions." Save this new channel by clicking Submit.

Each print edition only needs a title and nothing else, so we will create a new custom field group called "Print Editions" but not add any other fields. ExpressionEngine will, by default, display only the Title and URL Title fields. In the future, however, we can expand the print edition entry with more data about the edition (a PDF of the front page, for example) by adding other fields.

With the new channel created, let's add a couple of print editions to ExpressionEngine. Click the Content button in the main navigation, choose Publish, and then choose Print Editions. For the title, we'll use a full date, like March 1, 2010. After entering the title, save the entry. Create one more for March 2, 2010.

The next step is to create a way to relate each news article with a print edition. We'll do this by creating a new custom field in the News Articles custom field group.

Navigate to the Custom Channel Fields page using the Admin button in the main navigation. The custom field group we want to edit is News Articles. Click the red "Add/Edit Custom Fields" text next to New Articles to edit the custom channel fields.

We need to create one field for relating a news article entry to a print edition entry. Click Create a New Custom Field at the top right. For the label, input "Print Edition," and for the Field Name use "print_edition." You can also give some brief instructions such as "Choose the print edition in which article appeared."

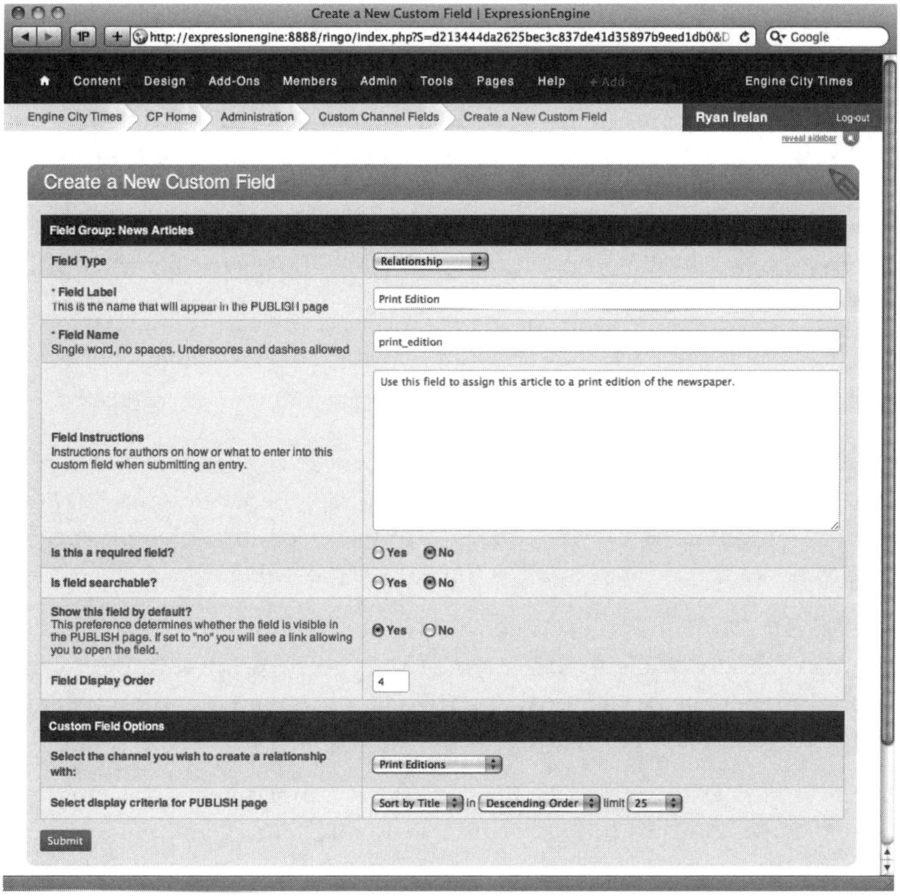

Figure 7.2: CREATING THE CUSTOM FIELD FOR THE RELATIONSHIP BETWEEN ENTRIES AND NEWS ARTICLES

As shown in Figure 7.2, on the previous page, the field type we need to choose is Relationship. After selecting that field type from the top of the form, some new options will appear under the Custom Field Options area. First, we need to choose with which channel we'd like to create the relationship. We want to relate to the print editions, so choose that channel. The defaults for sorting are fine, but we do want to adjust the limit to the last twenty-five. This will help keep the menu from becoming too long and unwieldy. Click Submit to save the new field.

With the relationship field created, let's view it in the publish form. Go to the Edit Channel Entries page using the Content button in the main navigation. Choose a recent news article, and scroll down to the new Print Edition field. Choose a date, and save the entry. Do this for one more news article entry so we have some entries to play with while adding the necessary template code.

7.3 Writing Related Entries Template Code

With the content channels set up and the necessary custom fields created, we have the ability to create relationships between entries. However, we still have some work to do. We now need to use some special tags to make those relationships appear on the website.

The *Engine City Times* requested that readers be able to browse articles by print edition. We will add a list of the recent print editions to the sidebar (under the search box) and then create a template that displays all the news articles related to that print edition.

The first step is to create the print editions template group. Using the Design navigation button, go to the Template Manager. Create a new template group called "print_editions." ExpressionEngine will automatically create the index template. We need only one template, so we will use the "index" to display our print editions.

Open the template-print-editions.html file from the code bundle you downloaded from this book's web page. You may notice that it is very similar to the category template we used earlier in the book in Section 5.5, *Lighting Up the Category Template*, on page 89.

Paste the template code into the index template in the print_editions template group. Go ahead and use the existing embed templates to make the template work like templates we created earlier.

Think of this template as the individual entry template we created for the news articles; its job is to display the content of a single entry. In this case, it will be the content of an entry in the print_editions channel.

We'll start just below the div with the id of print-edition-articles. Since the primary content is from the print_editions channel, we need to add a Channel Entries tag pair around everything inside the div. We'll remove the hard-coded date and replace it with the title variable. By leaving the "Print Edition" text there, the following code will display the title as, for example, "March 1, 2010 Print Edition":

RelatedEntries/print-edition-1.html

```
<div id="print-edition-articles">
 {exp:channel:entries channel="print_editions"
  disable="pagination" limit="1"}
 <h3>{title} Print Edition</h3>
   ...
 {/exp:channel:entries}
</div><!-- END #print-edition-articles -->
```

Just like we did with the markup in the categories template in Section 5.5, *Lighting Up the Category Template*, on page 89, we'll remove all but one instance of the divs with the lcol, mcol, and rcol ids.

Around the div, we place our Reverse Related Entries tag pair. Here's what the tag pair looks like:

```
{reverse_related_entries sort="desc"
 status="Open|Top Story|Featured Top Story"}
  ...
{/reverse_related_entries}
```

This tag pair has to live in the Channel Entries tag pair in order to work. We're using two parameters: sort and status. The sort parameter has the value of desc, so ExpressionEngine will display the entries by date in descending order. Since we're using custom statuses, we also have to tell ExpressionEngine which status the entries should have.

Along with the switch tag to make the columns appear properly, we'll add the Reverse Related Entries tag pair into our template. That part of the template should now look like this:

RelatedEntries/print-edition-2.html

```
<div id="print-edition-articles">
{exp:channel:entries channel="print_editions"
 disable="pagination" limit="1"}
```

```
<h3>{title} Print Edition</h3>

{reverse_related_entries sort="desc"
status="Open|Top Story|Featured Top Story"}
<div id="{switch="lcol|mcol|rcol"}">
 <h4>{title}</h4>
 <h5><span class="by">By</span> {author}</h5>
 {article_excerpt}
 <p><a href="{title_permalink="news_articles/view"}"
      class="read_story">Read Story</a></p>
    </div>
{/reverse_related_entries}

{/exp:channel:entries}
</div><!-- END #print-edition-articles -->
```

The Reverse Related Entries tag pair uses standard Channel Entries tag pair variables, including custom field variables. So, displaying the article title, author, excerpt, and permalink should be very familiar.

To finish this template, let's make the document title also reflect the print edition being viewed. We will add the title parameter to the document_header embed template and then use a Channel Entries tag pair to pull in the title. The code looks like this:

RelatedEntries/print-edition-header.html

```
{embed="includes/document_header"
title="{exp:channel:entries channel="print_editions"
disable="pagination" limit="1"} {title} Print
Edition{/exp:channel:entries}"}
```

The completed template should look similar to the page in Figure 7.3, on the facing page.

The only thing left to implement is a simple listing of the five most recent print editions in the sidebar of the *Engine City Times* website. By now you should be well prepared to take on this simple task, so how about some homework?

Using the code available in the download bundle from this book's web-page, add the list to the sidebar template, and light it up with the Channel Entries tag pair.

7.4   What We Learned

Creating print editions for the *Engine City Times* website is only one example of what you can do with entry relationships in ExpressionEn-

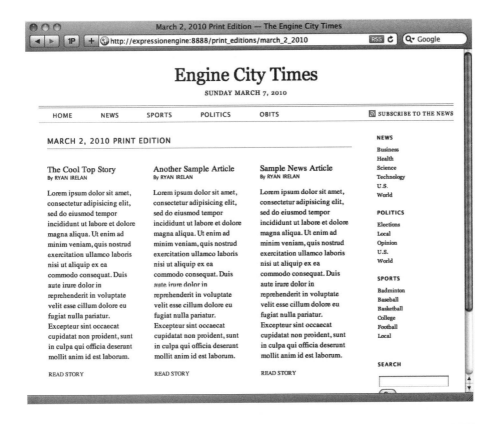

Figure 7.3: VIEWING THE PRINT EDITION PAGE

gine. As you build more and more ExpressionEngine-powered websites, you'll find related entries to be an essential tool. Entry relationships allow you to better organize and display more complex data and content in a way that is easy to manage.

Moving forward, we're going to learn even more skills to help you master ExpressionEngine: file management skills, advanced templating techniques, and more. Onward!

Chapter 8

Managing Files and Images

Content management systems like ExpressionEngine allow you to manage both content and assets (such as images and PDF's) all within an easy-to-use interface in your web browser. But it wasn't always so easy. Back before the widespread availability and use of free and affordable content management systems, it was much more manual. If you wanted to include an image on a page, you would upload it via FTP and then add the markup to the HTML file to make the image appear. This wasn't a difficult process, but it did make it harder for nontechnical people to easily update the site content.

In this chapter, you'll learn to use the File Manager, a new feature in ExpressionEngine 2, and set it up as a powerful and easy way to manage files and assets. You will also learn how to upload different types of content using file upload destinations, which are collections of preferences that tell ExpressionEngine where to save the file, what type of file is allowed, and more. Once you have your files uploaded, you'll embed them in entries and make them available in the *Engine City Times* article template.

8.1 Exploring the File Manager

Before we start setting up our file uploads, let's first get an overview of the File Manager. In the Control Panel, click the Content button, and then select File Manager. The File Manager should look sparse because we haven't uploaded any files or set up additional upload destinations.

On the left side is the file list that is grouped by upload directory. The default destination, Main Upload Directory, is already there. When we upload files, they will appear in the table, which is divided into

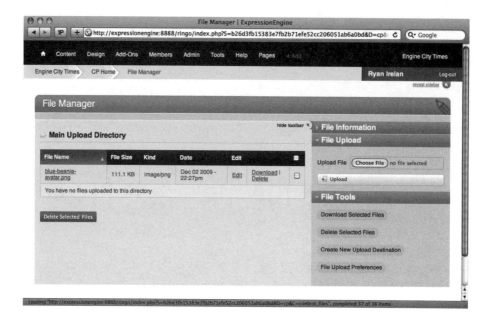

Figure 8.1: AFTER UPLOADING A FILE TO THE FILE MANAGER, IT APPEARS
IN THE LIST.

six columns. The first five columns can be sorted by clicking the column header. The last column is used to toggle the checkboxes that will appear next to each file listing.

Let's upload a file to the Main Upload Directory. On the right side of the File Manager, click File Upload to expose the upload form. Choose a small image from your computer. Once you select the file, the File Manager will automatically upload the file, and it will appear in the file list under Main Upload Directory, as shown in Figure 8.1.

The file table contains some information about each file you have uploaded. You also have a few links you can click to take action on the file. To preview the file, click the filename (in the first column), and you should see a small window appear with a preview of the image. Click the X to close the preview. The preview will only work with image files (JPG, JPEG PNG, GIF).

When you selected the file, more information about the file, including the file permissions, appeared under the File Information section on the right side of the File Manager. Below the File Upload section is the File

Tools section, where you can delete or download multiple files. When multiple files are downloaded, the File Manager places them in a directory called image and compress it into a ZIP file before downloading.

Below the download and delete options, there are two links to assist in creating new upload destinations and managing the file upload preferences, where you can manage existing upload destinations.

Now that we have a quick overview of what the File Manager looks like, let's move forward and create a new file upload destination. After that, we will start uploading files and displaying or making them available on the *Engine City Times* website.

8.2 Creating and Managing Upload Destinations

The first step to managing files with the File Manager is to set up the upload destinations. The upload destinations allow you define where ExpressionEngine should save the file, the type of file allowed, the file size limit, and more. You can also restrict an upload destination to a one or more member groups.

You can set up as many upload destinations as necessary. For the *Engine City Times* website, we'll create one for news article images and one for downloadable PDF files of the article. The first thing we need to do is decide where to save the files.

Creating the Upload Directories

Each upload destination requires that we set a physical location on our server where ExpressionEngine should upload and save the files. This can be anywhere on your server that ExpressionEngine can access. For files that you want to display or make available for download (like the images we'll use in the *Engine City Times*), the physical file location has to be in the public directory (the one where the ExpressionEngine application files live).

ExpressionEngine comes with a default upload destination called Main Upload Directory. Under File Tools, click File Upload Preferences to see a listing of the upload destinations. Click the Edit link for Main Upload Directory to see the preferences.

The second preference listed is Server Path to Upload Directory, and you can see that it is set to save the files in the uploads directory, which lives in the images directory in the root of the site. ExpressionEngine has this directory set up for us by default, but that doesn't mean we have to use it. For our *Engine City Times* file uploads, we want to save the files in the site root in a directory. However, ExpressionEngine will not automatically create those directories. We have to do that.

On the server, in the root of the website, use an FTP client to create two directories: article_images and article_pdfs. One directory is for the article images, and one is to store the PDFs. Using your FTP program, check that the permissions of the directories we just created are set to 777 on Mac OS X and Unix or to Writeable on Windows. By doing this, we ensure that the directories have the proper permissions to allow ExpressionEngine to save the files.

You should now have two directories in the root of your site: article_images and article_pdfs. Remember those two directory names because we'll need them in the next step when we create the new file upload destinations.

Creating the File Upload Destinations

With the new directories created, we are now ready to create the file upload destinations that ExpressionEngine will use to manage our files.

Navigate to the File Manager in the Control Panel by clicking the Content button and selecting File Manager. Under File Tools, click the Create New Upload Destination link. We have two destinations to create, but let's do the one for the article images first.

We're presented with a form (see Figure 8.2, on the facing page) to create the new destination. First we want to name the destination; let's keep it simple and name ours "Article Images." The name can be anything, but it's important to keep it descriptive so the people uploading the files know which destination to use. Next, we need to set the path to the upload directory we created earlier in Section 8.2, *Creating the Upload Directories*, on the previous page. ExpressionEngine prefills the server path to the ExpressionEngine installation, so we just need to append our article_images directory after the last forward slash. The file path (which will be different on every server) should look something like this: /path/to/ee/article_images.

The next step is to define the URL where the files will be accessible. ExpressionEngine will use this URL to display the image in the template. Since we placed our article_images directory in the site root, creating the URL of the upload directory is as simple as appending arti-

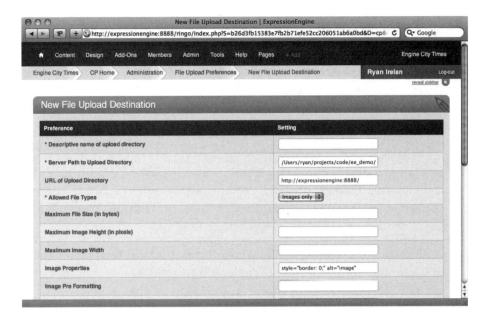

Figure 8.2: ADDING A NEW FILE UPLOAD DESTINATION

cle_images to the end of the site URL that ExpressionEngine prefills for us. So, your upload directory URL should look something like this: http://mysite.com/article_images.

There are several more preferences we can set. Here's a rundown of what's available:

- *Allowed File Types*: There are two options: Images Only and All File Types. We want to use Images Only for this destination because we'll only be uploading images for the news articles. While All File Types includes everything, Images Only will allow certain image files to be upload. They must be of the type PNG, GIF, JPG, or JPEG. Any other image types will be refused.

- *Maximum File Size*: Entered in bytes, the value of this field will let you restrict the upload file size. For a 1MB file limit, you would enter 1048576 (bytes). Let's set that for this upload destination. This should be more than enough for the news article images.

- *Maximum Image Height and Maximum Image Width*: The next two fields allow you to restrict the height and width in pixels of the upload image. News article images for the *Engine City Times* will be of varying size, so we will leave these two preferences blank.

- *Image Properties*: Here you can set any properties in the img tag, like style and alt. By default ExpressionEngine includes a style to remove borders around images and alt text. You can also use this to give the img element a class or id so the image is easier to style using CSS.

- *Image Pre Formatting and Image Post Formatting*: If you need to add markup before or after the image (like wrapping it in a containing div), these two preferences will be very handy. We can leave both fields blank for the news article images.

- *File Properties*: Just like the Image Properties preference, this allows you to set properties to the anchor link that appears for non-image files. Since we're using only images in this destination, we will leave this blank.

- *File Pre Formatting and File Post Formatting*: This allows you to wrap file download links in any markup you want. It functions the same as the Image Pre Formatting and Image Post Formatting preference. This destination is only for images, so we can leave this field blank.

- *Restrict file uploading to select member groups*: The final setting before we create the new upload destination allows us to determine who is and is not allowed to upload files to this destination. As a Super Admin, you are always allowed to upload files. We don't, however, want Members to be able to upload files, so toggle that to No.

With all of the preferences set, click Submit to add the news articles destination to ExpressionEngine.

Navigate back to the File Manager. You should now see the Article Images upload destination listed above the Main Upload Directory destination. There aren't files listed because we haven't uploaded any! Using the File Upload tool on the right side of the File Manager, upload a few test files to make sure everything is working OK.

On Your Own

The editors of the *Engine City Times* would also like to offer downloadable PDF versions of some of the new articles on the website. Now that you know how to create a file upload destination in ExpressionEngine, create another one for the PDFs of news articles. Since the destination will contain nonimage files, you want to make sure you allow that. Give the destination a short descriptive name like "Article PDFs."

After you create the new file upload destination for the PDFs, test that everything is working properly by uploading some PDFs in the File Manager. When you're done, you should have three upload destinations: Main Upload Directory, Articles Images, and the one you just created called Article PDFs.

Now that we have our file upload destinations created and some sample files uploaded, let's make some use of the image files by editing them in ExpressionEngine and then including them in a news article.

8.3   Editing Image Files

The File Manager also allows you to edit images directly in the Control Panel. The tools are simple but useful; you can do quick image cropping, resizing, and rotating. It could be especially useful to people who don't have dedicated image-editing software on their computer. For our *Engine City Times* website, the editing functionality gives reporters and editors the ability to quickly edit photos for the news articles. Let's take a look at the different features of the image editor.

To access the editing screen, choose an image from your list of files, and click the Edit link in the fifth column of the table. If the Edit link does not appear for a file, that means it is not a file type that ExpressionEngine can edit. Only the acceptable image formats (PNG, GIF, JPG, and JPEG) will be available to edit in the File Manager.

After clicking Edit for an image, you are brought to the Edit screen of the File Manager. On the left is the image that you'll be editing. On the right are the three different edit modes available: crop, resize, and rotate.

Cropping an Image

Click the Crop Mode button to begin cropping an image. You should see a small animated outline box, like in Figure 8.3, on the following page. Use your mouse to resize, and move the box to set your crop. On the right side, the crop values will change as you move and resize the outlined box. You can also set those crop values manually if you already know exactly the crop you need.

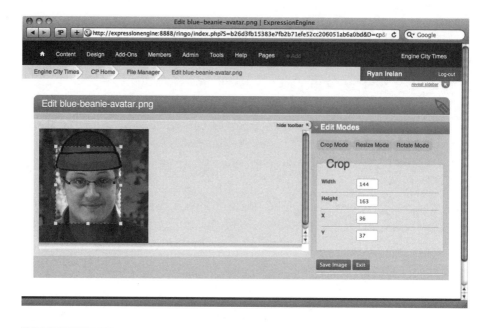

Figure 8.3: CROPPING AN IMAGE IN THE FILE MANAGER

Once you have the crop you like, click Save Image to save the changes. The image editor should reload and display the updated, cropped image. There is no undo for cropping, so make sure you are satisfied before saving the edit!

Resizing an Image

If an image is cropped as you like, you may still want to resize it so it fits properly within the design of the website. Choose an image to edit, and then click the Resize Mode button. Two input boxes will appear containing the current dimensions of the image. Adjust either the width or height, and the other value will also change to keep the image constrained to its original proportions. But be careful; sizing the image up (increasing the width and height) may cause loss of quality.

To save the resized image, click Save Image.

Rotating an Image

The last edit option is Rotate Mode, which allows you to change the orientation of the image. Click the Rotate Mode button, and a box with four rotate options should appear. The first option lets you rotate the image to the right, and the second rotates the images to the left. The last two options allow you to flip the image top to bottom (turning it upside down) and right to left (reversing the image).

Take a few minutes to play around with the four different rotating buttons, and when you have your image as you like it, click Save Image to save the image.

If you work with a lot of images accompanying content, you will quickly find great value in having a simple image editor right inside the ExpressionEngine Control Panel. The ability to resize, crop, and rotate images will save you from having to launch bulky image-editing software for simple tasks. Even better, you don't have to leave the Control Panel.

Now that we have our images edited and ready for the site, let's learn how to embed images directly in our entries.

8.4 Embedding Images in Entries

ExpressionEngine makes it simple to embed an image you uploaded through the File Manager and have it appear in the content of an entry. If you didn't upload images earlier in the chapter, you should add some now before going further. If you have image uploaded in the File Manager, then let's get started embedding.

Embedding images in entries is the most common usage. For the *Engine City Times* website, we will create a new news article and embed an image in it.

Click the Content button at the top of the Control Panel, select Publish, and then select News Articles. Create a sample entry (give it any title you please), adding a short excerpt and some content in the article body.

Above the Article Body textarea is a formatting toolbar (see Figure 8.4, on the next page). The second-to-last icon, which looks like an image of a tree, is what we want to use to embed an image in the article body.

Place your cursor in the middle of the content, just to the left of the first letter of a sentence, and then click the image icon in the formatting toolbar. An overlay should appear that displays a form to upload a new image or to choose an image from one of your file upload destination. Choose Main Upload Directory, and then select the image you want to

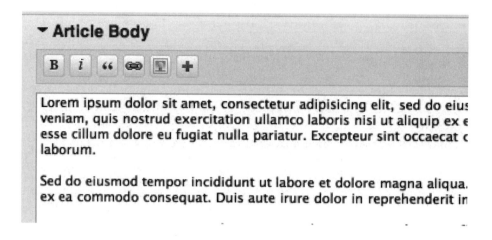

Figure 8.4: Using the toolbar to embed an image in the field content

embed by clicking it. ExpressionEngine should add the img element at the beginning of the content in the article body.

Save the entry, and then view the article on the *Engine City Times* website. It should look something like Figure 8.5, on the facing page. The image appears in the flow of the content of the article, and the text wraps nicely around it.

If you want to apply any styles to the image, you can use the file upload destination preferences we set back in Section 8.2, *Creating the File Upload Destinations*, on page 126 to add properties to the img element. Use the properties to include inline styles or to add a CSS class or id. This would be useful if you wanted to add a border around the image, increase padding or margins, or set the image on a colored background.

Embedding images is a great way to break up large chunks of text in an entry and give the reader something to look at. However, there is another way to include files with an entry—but not right in the content field—and it's done using a custom file upload field.

8.5 Adding Files to Entries

While viewing the *Engine City Times* article you just created in the previous section, you probably saw that the article still had the gray placeholder image with the text "news article image."

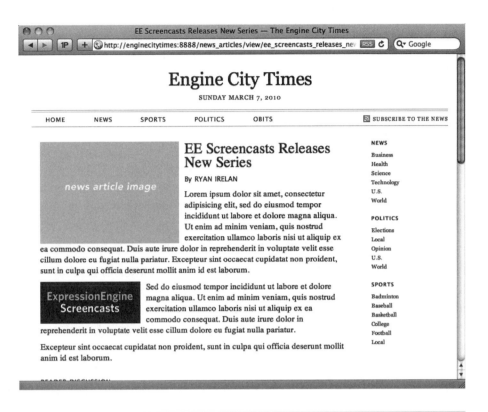

Figure 8.5: VIEWING THE EMBEDDED IMAGE ON THE WEBSITE

We weren't able to address this image using embedded images because it lives outside the entry content. Let's take a quick look at a snippet of the markup for the news articles:

FileManagement/article-view.html

```
<div id="content">
 <div id="article">
 <img src="/img/news-article-image.png"
        alt="News Article Image" />
 <h4>EE Screencasts Releases New Series</h4>
 <h5><span class="by">By</span> Ryan Irelan</h5>
     <p>Lorem ipsum ...</p>
```

The main image for the article lives outside the content area in a dedicated img element. To change this image, we have to somehow place an article-specific image in that img element. We could use a simple input field in our publish form and type the URL to the image (after we manually upload it to the server). Or we could allow the user to upload an image right in the form and have it attached to the entry. This is the better choice.

New to ExpressionEngine 2 is a native file upload field that you can place in the publish form for entries. It makes uploading and attaching files to entries very simple. We only need to add a new custom field and tell ExpressionEngine where to upload the file.

Adding the Upload Field

In the Control Panel, click the Admin button, then Channel Administration, and finally Custom Fields. Click Add/Edit Custom Fields for the News Articles field group. Create a new field, giving it the label "Article Image" and the short name "article_image." From the Field Type list, choose Upload, and then choose Image from the File Type select list. Click Submit to save the new field.

Bring up the edit form for the article we created earlier in Section 8.4, *Embedding Images in Entries*, on page 131, and you should see the new Article Image upload field. Click Choose File, and select an image to attach to the entry. You can also choose which upload destination should be used; the Article Images destination should be selected by default. Click Submit to save the changes and upload the file.

The image won't yet appear with the article because we haven't updated our template with the new field. Let's do that now.

Adjusting the Article View Template

When we attached and uploaded a new article image to the new article entry, ExpressionEngine did not actually save the image in the entry. ExpressionEngine uploaded the file to our Article Image upload destination and then saved the URL to that image in the entry Upload field. This makes it easy for us for drop the field variable in the src property of the img element in the view template (located in the news_articles template group). Let's look at that bit of template code:

FileManagement/article-view.html

```
<div id="content">
 <div id="article">
 {exp:channel:entries channel="news_articles" limit="1"
  status="Open|Top Story|Featured Top Story"}
 <img src="/img/news-article-image.png"
      alt="News Article Image" />
  <h4>{title}</h4>
```

We just need to drop in the field variable for the image, article_image, replacing the /img/news-article-image.png path with the variable.

The template code should now look like this:

```
FileManagement/article-view.html

<div id="content">
 <div id="article">
 {exp:channel:entries channel="news_articles" limit="1"
  status="Open|Top Story|Featured Top Story"}
 <img src="{article_image}" alt="News Article Image" />
  <h4>{title}</h4>
```

Save the template, and then view the article again on the *Engine City Times* website. If your code is set up correctly, you should now see the image you uploaded with the news article.

We now have given the editors and reporters at the *Engine City Times* the ability to attach an article image that will appear to the left of the headline.

On Your Own

Back in Section 8.2, *Creating the Upload Directories*, on page 125, we created an upload destination for PDF files to be included with the articles. The *Engine City Times* staff will be creating downloadable versions of the articles and making them available as PDF files.

On your own, enable this functionality for the *Engine City Times* website by setting up a new Upload custom field and then placing a link at the bottom of the article where the reader can download the file. Not every article will have a PDF file, so you'll want to use a simple conditional to check whether there is one available before displaying the HTML to create the download link. Good luck!

8.6 What We Learned

In this chapter, we learned how to manage images and files using the ExpressionEngine File Manager. We were able to embed an image directly in the content of a news article on the *Engine City Times* website. For files that we didn't embed in the content, we used the Upload custom field type to attach files directly to the entry. This allowed us to make the images appear wherever we wanted.

We've been spending a lot of time working in the Control Panel, so let's change over to working in the templates. In the next chapter, we'll learn some advanced templating techniques that will help us make our ExpressionEngine templates more powerful and useful.

Chapter 9

Advanced Templating

In the previous part, we built the *Engine City Times* website from beginning to end. Throughout the process, we learned all the basic skills needed to build websites with ExpressionEngine. Now we'll add to that knowledge and get closer to becoming ExpressionEngine experts who can tackle almost any ExpressionEngine website project.

In this chapter, we'll learn some advanced templating techniques that give us finer control over how we present content to the user. We'll learn how the user can submit content to the site using a stand-alone entry form. We'll see how to create a more powerful Channel Entries tag using two new parameters: dynamic_parameters and search. Finally, we'll explore how to display any data we want with custom MySQL queries, right in an ExpressionEngine template.

9.1 A More Powerful Channel Entries Tag

By now we're familiar with the Channel Entries tag and how to use it in a template to display content. Well, it can do even more. Let's take a step forward and improve our templating skills and what we can do with the Channel Entries tag. We'll learn how to search inside custom fields and dynamically set the Channel Entries tag parameters.

Searching Inside Custom Fields

The first power tip for the Channel Entries tag is to use the search: parameter, which allows us to display content that matches some content in our custom fields.

We use it like this:

AdvancedTemplating/search-custom-fields.html

```
{exp:channel:entries channel="site" search:body="pig"}

  {title}

{/exp:channel:entries}
```

In the example, we're using the search: parameter to tell Expression-Engine to search in the body field of all entries in the site channel and display the titles of those entries where "pig" is in the body field. This is useful in the *Engine City Times* website to show all news articles that mention, for example, "Obama" in the body of an article. In that example, we use the search: parameter like this:

AdvancedTemplating/search-custom-fields.html

```
{exp:channel:entries channel="news_articles"
 search:article_body="Obama"}
 {title}
{/exp:channel:entries}
```

This code will return all articles that have the word "Obama" in the article_body custom field. The search: parameter also accepts multiple terms. You just need to separate them with the pipe character.

AdvancedTemplating/search-custom-fields.html

```
{exp:channel:entries channel="news_articles"
 search:article_body="Obama|Clinton"}
 {title}
{/exp:channel:entries}
```

The previous code will display all news articles where the article_body field contains either "Obama" or "Clinton." There is no limit to how many search terms you can use.

To return all news articles that contain both terms, separate the terms with a double ampersand instead of with a pipe:

AdvancedTemplating/search-custom-fields.html

```
{exp:channel:entries channel="news_articles"
search:article_body="Obama&&Clinton"}
   {title}
{/exp:channel:entries}
```

To match entries that do not contain a certain term, use the not term in the parameter value. So, instead of search:article_body="Obama" as the parameter value, the value to return all entries that *do not* contain the word "Obama" in the article body would be search:article_body="not Obama".

We can further refine our searches using two more special parameter values: an = sign for exact searches and IS_EMPTY to check whether the custom field is empty.

To do exact matching of a term, we prepend the search term with the = sign:

AdvancedTemplating/search-custom-fields.html

```
{exp:channel:entries channel="site"
 search:body="=pig"}
  {title}
{/exp:channel:entries}
```

This only displays entries where "pig" is the *only* word in the body field. This isn't useful for large content fields (like the news_body field in the *Engine City Times*) but could come in handy if we wanted to match entries from a job database that contained a job title in the field, like "News Editor."

AdvancedTemplating/search-custom-fields.html

```
{exp:channel:entries channel="jobs"
 search:job_title="=News Editor"}
  {title}
{/exp:channel:entries}
```

The code returns all entries in the jobs channel where the job_title field contains exactly "News Editor" and nothing else.

If we didn't use the exact matching and we had an entry with the job title "Editor in Chief," that job would also be returned in the results. To get the correct results, we have to prepend = to the search term.

We can also check whether fields contain no content. To display job listings where no salary has been specified (by leaving the salary field blank), we use the special search constant IS_EMPTY.

AdvancedTemplating/search-custom-fields.html

```
{exp:channel:entries channel="jobs"
search:job_salary="IS_EMPTY"}
  {title}
{/exp:channel:entries}
```

In this code we search the jobs channel for all entries where the job_salary field is empty. ExpressionEngine returns all of the entries where the job_salary field has no content.

Dynamically Set Channel Entries

As we built the *Engine City Times* website, we worked extensively with the Channel Entries tag and its parameters. Up until this point, we've set the parameters right in the template; if we wanted to pull from the site channel, we assigned the channel parameter the value of site. ExpressionEngine displays entries from that channel until we change it in the template. That's how it normally works. However, using an advanced feature of the Channel Entries tag, we can allow the website visitor to change the values of the parameters. This feature in ExpressionEngine is called *dynamic parameters*, and it is yet another way we can make our ExpressionEngine templates even more powerful and customizable.

Dynamic parameters are a documented, yet rarely used, feature of ExpressionEngine that allow us to dynamically set any of the available Channel Entries tag pair parameters (there are more than forty to choose from). It gives users the flexibility to choose how they want the content to be presented. Let's use dynamic parameters to add some new functionality to the *Engine City Times* website.

We want to give readers the ability to control how many articles appear on the News page. Our goal is to present the reader with a simple drop-down menu, from which they choose a number from 1 to 10 and then click the Submit to alter the number of entries being displayed.

With dynamic parameters, we set the parameters using the POST data from a form. We will post the data using a simple form, like this:

AdvancedTemplating/dynamic-parameters.html
```
<form action="{path='news_articles/page/category/news'}"
        method="post">
 <select name="limit" id="limit">
  <option value="1">1</option>
  <option value="2">2</option>
  <option value="3">3</option>
  <option value="4">4</option>
  <option value="5">5</option>
  <option value="6">6</option>
  <option value="7">7</option>
  <option value="8">8</option>
  <option value="9">9</option>
  <option value="10">10</option>
 </select>
 <p><input type="submit" value="Submit"></p>
</form>
```

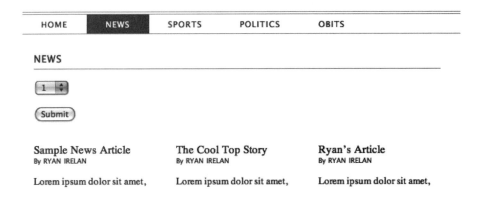

Figure 9.1: Dynamic parameters form to change number of articles on category page

This is a simple select option list with options from 1 to 10 and a Submit button to send the form data. Note two important things about the form:

- The name of the select element has to be the name of the parameter you want to dynamically set.
- The values of the options have to be the values you want to set to the parameter.

We want the form to submit to the same page the user is viewing (to keep this example simple, we're using the News category page), so we set the action of the form using the {path} variable.

Let's add the form to the top of the category template, just under the category name, so it looks like Figure 9.1.

Select a number from the drop-down, and click Submit. The page reloads, but the number of articles displayed doesn't change. Why? We still need to add a parameter to the Channel Entries tag pair that makes the three columns of articles appear. Add the dynamic_parameters parameter to the Channel Entries tag pair, like this:

AdvancedTemplating/dynamic-parameters.html

```
{exp:channel:entries channel="news_articles"
 limit="3" status="Open|Top Story|Featured Top Story"
 dynamic_parameters="limit"}

...

{/exp:channel:entries}
```

> **Joe Asks...**
>
> **How Do I Comment Out ExpressionEngine Code?**
>
> HTML commenting such as this lets you keep commented code or text from appearing in the browser:
>
> ```
> <!-- comment or code here -->
> ```
>
> ExpressionEngine, however, does not honor the HTML comment tags. If you place ExpressionEngine code inside the standard HTML comment tags, ExpressionEngine will still parse that code.
>
> To keep ExpressionEngine from parsing commented code, you have to use a special ExpressionEngine comment format, like:
>
> ```
> {!-- comment goes here --}
> ```

The dynamic_parameters parameter has a value of limit, which tells ExpressionEngine to dynamically set that parameter when the form is submitted and the page loads. For example, if we select 4 from the drop-down and click Submit, ExpressionEngine will set the limit parameter to 4 and display the page with four articles.

More than forty parameters are available in the Channel Entries tag pair, and we can dynamically set any of them. For example, use the author_id parameter to dynamically filter content based on the author, or use the category parameter to filter content by category. We can also set multiple parameters by separating them with a pipe:

AdvancedTemplating/dynamic-parameters.html

```
{exp:channel:entries channel="news_articles"
 limit="3" status="Open|Top Story|Featured Top Story"
 dynamic_parameters="limit|author_id"}

...

{/exp:channel:entries}
```

This code allows us to filter by author_id *and* limit.

9.2 Writing Custom MySQL Queries

Sometimes the tags provided by ExpressionEngine don't retrieve the data you need or do it in a way that is not useful to you. In these cases, you can use the Query module, which comes with paid versions of ExpressionEngine (in other words, not in the trial version) and allows you to easily write custom MySQL queries right in your templates.

To use the Query module effectively, you should have a basic knowledge of how to query for data in MySQL and a general understanding of the database schema used in ExpressionEngine. Basic MySQL querying isn't difficult to learn, and with a good reference book[1] or website,[2] you could pick it up in an afternoon.

To demonstrate how the Query module works and keep the query as simple as possible, we'll write query that displays the latest three news article titles. (Of course, this is available by using the Channel Entries tag pair.)

The Query module uses a tag pair that looks like this:

AdvancedTemplating/custom-queries.html
```
{exp:query sql="query here"}
 ...
{/exp:query}
```

The value of the sql parameter is the query you want use to retrieve data from the ExpressionEngine database. In between the tag pair is where you will return any results. Here's a simple query to retrieve the latest three news article titles:

AdvancedTemplating/custom-queries.html
```
{exp:query sql="SELECT title FROM exp_channel_titles
 WHERE channel_id = 6 LIMIT 3"}
  {title}<br />
{/exp:query}
```

The Query module handily returns the column name (in this case "title") as the name of the variable used to display the data in the template. Let's select another column:

AdvancedTemplating/custom-queries.html
```
{exp:query sql="SELECT title, url_title
 FROM exp_channel_titles WHERE channel_id = 6 LIMIT 3"}
<a href="http://yoursite.com/news_articles/view/{url_title}">
        {title}</a><br />
{/exp:query}
```

1. *MySQL Tutorial* by Luke Welling and Laura Thomson
2. http://dev.mysql.com

The Cool Top Story
Ryan's Article
Another Sample Article

Figure 9.2: RESULTS OF CUSTOM QUERY USING THE QUERY MODULE

In this example, we've also selected the url_title column from the database, which gives us the URI of the entry. To display this, we just use
the name of the column surrounded by curly braces, which gives us a
normal ExpressionEngine variable. Make sure to hyperlink the article
title by adding the URL to the view template in the news_articles template
group with the url_title variable at the end so it links to the proper article,
like in Figure 9.2

The following are a couple of useful special variables that come with the
Query module:

- {count}: This returns the count of the current result. If you have
  four results, the value of {count} for the first one will be 1, the
  second one 2, and so on.

- {total_results}: This returns the total number of results for the query.
  This is used in conjunction with {count} to determine when to
  insert markup (like the closing tag of a div or other container).

The Query module, although useful, only allows you to do SELECTs,
which are read-only. You cannot do UPDATEs or DELETEs or modify the
data in the database in any way. If you do find yourself with a need to
update or delete database records, you should use PHP in your template
or consider a custom module. I will cover this in Chapter 11, *Extend-*

ing ExpressionEngine with Add-Ons, on page 169. Adding data to the database from a template, however, is possible with the stand-alone entry form.

9.3 Adding Content Outside of the Control Panel

Throughout this chapter we've learned how to make our templates more dynamic and powerful when presenting content to visitors. Now we're going to move away from presenting content and learn how to allow visitors to *add* content, outside of the Control Panel, to the *Engine City Times* website.

You can do this using the stand-alone entry form (SAEF). This is a special form in ExpressionEngine that lets you display custom fields to a logged-in user to be filled out and submitted to the ExpressionEngine database as entries. For example, you could allow visitors to add a job posting to a job board website or add a classified ad to a website. To see a real-world implementation of an SAEF, visit the EE Insider Tips section of the EE Insider website.[3] It allows the ExpressionEngine community to easily submit and share their favorite ExpressionEngine tips and tricks.

You'll recall that back in Chapter 5, *Making the Pages*, on page 67 we added the Letters to the Editor section on the front page of the *Engine City Times* website. We entered the letters into ExpressionEngine using the Control Panel interface.

To demonstrate how to build an SAEF, we're going to implement a way for registered users to send letters to the editor and have those submitted letters added to ExpressionEngine with a status of "closed." We're using that status so a letter doesn't appear on the website until an editor has reviewed and approved it.

As you can see in Figure 9.3, on the following page, the Submit a Letter to the Editor form consists of only two fields: Subject and Your Thoughts. The Subject field is actually the entry title, and the Your Thoughts field is just a custom field to hold the letter body.

Before we get into the template code used, we need to create the template itself. Under the site template group, create a template called "letter_form," and save it.

---

3. http://eeinsider.com/tips

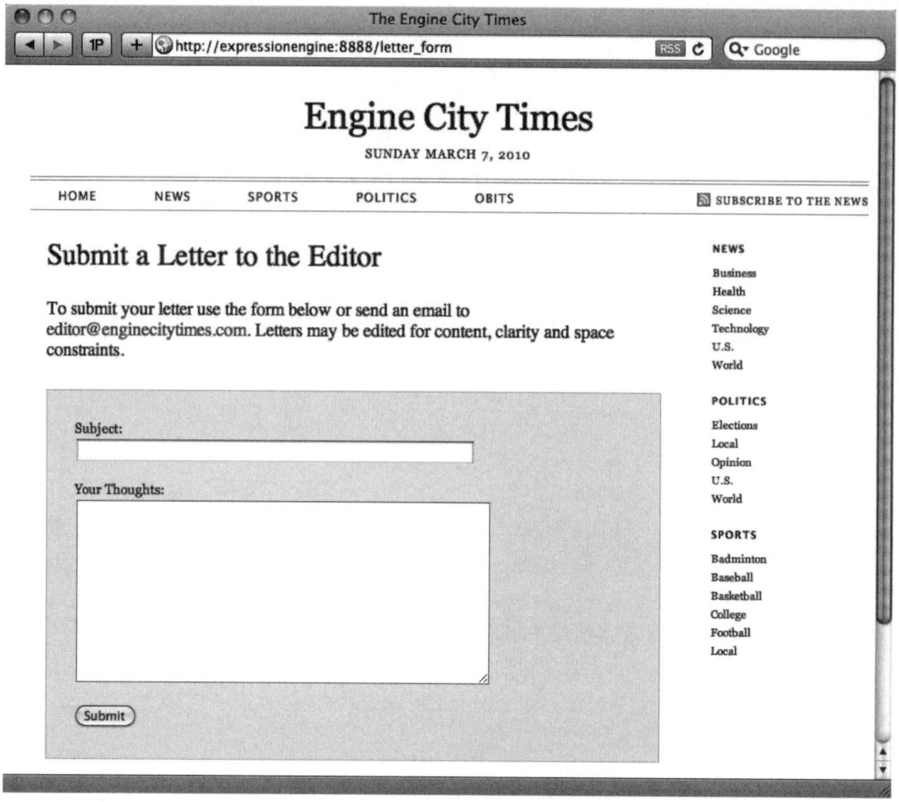

Figure 9.3: LETTER TO EDITOR SUBMISSION FORM

In the downloaded directory of site template files, open letter_form.html, copy the entire contents of the file into the newly created letter_form template, and save it. Add the appropriate embed templates to make the template the same as others in the site.

We're going to focus on the form itself. Right now it's just typical form code; there's an input field, a textarea, and a submit button.

AdvancedTemplating/saef.html

```
<form action="saef-form-form" method="post" accept-charset="utf-8">

 <p><label for="Subject">Subject:</label><br /><input
type="text" name="" value="" id="" size="50"/></p>

 <p><label for="letter-content">Your Thoughts:</label>
<br /><textarea name="Name" rows="10" cols="50"></textarea></p>

  <p><input type="submit" value="Submit"></p>
</form>
```

As you can see, the action doesn't go anywhere, so we need to light up this form so it submits content to the letter_to_editor section in ExpressionEngine. We'll do this using the SAEF tags that ExpressionEngine provides.

Adding SAEF Tags to the Form

The first step to creating an SAEF is to replace the form tags with the special SAEF tags that ExpressionEngine gives us.

First, locate the opening tag of the form:

AdvancedTemplating/saef.html

```
<form action="saef-form-form" method="post"
    accept-charset="utf-8">
```

and completely replace it with the SAEF tag:

AdvancedTemplating/saef.html

```
{exp:channel:entry_form channel="letters_to_editor"
return="site/thank_you" status="Closed"}
```

The tag pair takes a few parameters we need to set. The first is channel, which, like the Channel Entries tag pair, tells ExpressionEngine which section to use. In this case, we're telling ExpressionEngine which section to add to the submitted form data. The second parameter is return, which tells ExpressionEngine where to direct the user after the form is successfully submitted. The third parameter is status, which allows you to set the status of the new entry. The editors of the *Engine City Times* would like to edit and approve all letters to the editor that appear on the site, so we'll give the status of "closed" to any letter submitted with the form.

Let's continue bringing the form to life. Find the closing form tag:

```
</form>
```

and replace it with the closing SAEF tag:

```
{/exp:channel:entry_form}
```

Now we make some changes to the form elements (the input field and textarea) so they work with our SAEF. Let's start with the Subject field:

```
<input type="text" name="" value="" id="" size="50"/>
```

Since we're using the title field for the Subject, we need to give the name parameter the value of name and the value parameter the value of {title}, which is a variable ExpressionEngine will use to repopulate the field upon an incorrect form submission. With that done, the input field code should look like this:

`AdvancedTemplating/saef.html`

```
<input type="text" name="title" value="{title}"
        id="title" size="50"/>
```

To tackle the textarea, we employ a new tag pair, {custom_fields}, that is special to the SAEF. This tag pair will loop through every custom field of the field group assigned to the section and display them in the template. This makes it simple to use a small amount of code to generate several form fields. Since we have only one field, it will be even simpler.

Inside the {custom_fields} tag pair, we need to put in an if statement to check to see whether there are any textarea fields to display.

`AdvancedTemplating/saef.html`

```
{custom_fields}
{if textarea}
        ...
{/if}
{/custom_fields}
```

If there is a textarea (which there is for this form), we want to display the textarea markup. We also give the parameters values using special variables. ExpressionEngine will automatically assign the correct value for each parameter based on which textarea it is showing. This includes the {field_data} variable, which will repopulate the field with the submitted data if there was an error while submitting the form.

`AdvancedTemplating/saef.html`

```
{custom_fields}
{if textarea}
        <p><label for="letter-content">Your Thoughts:</label>
        <br />
        <textarea id="{field_name}" name="{field_name}"
                rows="{rows}" cols="50">{field_data}
        </textarea></p>
{/if}
{/custom_fields}
```

The complete form should look like this:

`AdvancedTemplating/saef.html`

```
{exp:channel:entry_form channel="letters_to_editor"
 return="site/thank_you" status="Closed"}

<p><label for="Subject">Subject:</label>
<br />
```

```
<input type="text" name="title" value="{title}"
        id="title" size="50"/></p>
        {custom_fields}
        {if textarea}
<p><label for="letter-content">Your Thoughts:</label>
<br />
<textarea id="{field_name}" name="{field_name}"
        rows="{rows}" cols="50">{field_data}</textarea></p>
        {/if}
        {/custom_fields}
<p><input type="submit" value="Submit"></p>
{/exp:channel:entry_form}
```

With the form in place, we have a small amount of cleanup work to do. If you were not logged in while working on this template, the SAEF did not appear. Next up, we'll handle this situation with a simple conditional.

Checking for a Logged-in User

Submitting the SAEF requires that the user is logged in to Expression-Engine. This could be as a normal user with no access to the Control Panel or as an administrator. If you are not logged in, the form will not appear. This is a security measure built in to ExpressionEngine to prevent unauthorized users from adding data to your ExpressionEngine database. We want to display some text for those users who try to access the SAEF when they're not logged in.

Right below the introductory text ("To submit your letter use..."), we'll add a conditional to check whether the user is logged out, and if so, we'll display some text.

`AdvancedTemplating/saef.html`

```
{if logged_out}
  <p>To submit a letter you must have a member account.
        Please <a href="{path=member/login}">log in</a>
        or <a href="{path=member/register}">sign up for
        a free account</a>.
  </p>
{/if}
```

After placing this in the template, sign out of the Control Panel, and then reload the page. You will see the text we just added (see Figure 9.4, on the next page).

Log back in to the Control Panel, and then reload the page to make the form appear again. Fill out the form with some sample data, and then submit it. It should submit properly and then redirect you to the

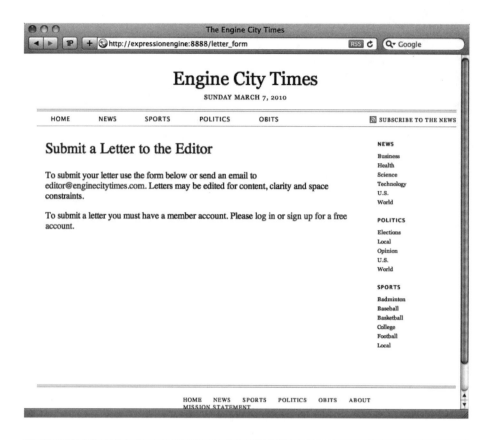

Figure 9.4: LETTER TO EDITOR SUBMISSION PAGE WHEN LOGGED OUT

thank_you template. We haven't created that template, but it's just a simple template thanking the user for submitting the letter.

Log in to the Control Panel, and check that the entry was added to the proper channel and has a status of "closed." If so, your SAEF is set up and working properly.

We've now created our first SAEF and enabled the *Engine City Times* visitors to submit letters directly to the website. This is just one example of how to use an SAEF. Think for a moment about other uses. What ideas do you have? Do you see how it can help you build websites that are more useful to your users?

9.4 Sharing Data Between Templates

In Chapter 5, *Making the Pages*, on page 67, we learned about sharing code across templates using embed templates. This keeps us from repeating the same code in multiple templates and makes managing and updating templates a lot easier (and faster). Used creatively, you can pare down the number of templates required to run a website.

But there's more to embed templates than just the templates themselves. The handiest part of embed templates is the embed variable functionality. Embed variables allow you to pass data from one template to another using special variables declared in your embed tag.

Why is this so useful? While building out the *Engine City Times* website in Chapter 5, *Making the Pages*, on page 67, we put the header code for the entire site in one file and embedded it in every template. We did this because updating one header file is easier than updating twenty. Our embed tag looks like this:

AdvancedTemplating/embed-variables.html

```
{embed="includes/document_header"}
```

To use an embed variable and share data from the main template to the embed template, you add a parameter with the name of the variable you'd like to pass to the document_header template. Give the variable any name you want, as long as it doesn't conflict with another variable in the embed template.

For the *Engine City Times* document_header template, we want to pass the page title, so we'll call the variable page_title.

AdvancedTemplating/embed-variables.html

```
{embed="includes/document_header" page_title=""}
```

Now we need to assign some data to the page_title variable. We need to find the page title (the title of the entry that is being viewed), so we'll use the standard Channel Entries tag pair. We can just place the entire tag pair plus its variable (in this case we're using the {title} variable) inside the double quotes of the {page_title} variable.

AdvancedTemplating/embed-variables.html

```
{embed="includes/document_header"
 page_title="{exp:channel:entries
  channel="news_articles" limit="1"}
  {title}{/exp:channel:entries}"}
```

This code works because ExpressionEngine parses the Channel Entries tag pair *before* the embed tag. When it comes time to parse the embed tag, the value of the page_title is already set with the title of the current entry.[4]

With the variable properly created and set, ExpressionEngine will embed the document_header template and pass along the current entry's title. In that template, we have all of the code for the header of our page. Here's a snippet of the template:

`AdvancedTemplating/embed-variables.html`

```
<head>
 <meta http-equiv="Content-Type" content="text/html;
  charset=utf-8"/>
 <title>The Engine City Times</title>
```

We want to customize the title tag so it also displays the title of whatever page or article that is currently being displayed. The title comes from the value of the embed variable that is being passed to the template.

Right now the document_head template only displays "The Engine City Times" for every page. We want to keep that as part of the title tag but also prepend the page title. To do this, we'll simply add the embed variable.

`AdvancedTemplating/embed-variables.html`

```
<head>
 <meta http-equiv="Content-Type" content="text/html;
 charset=utf-8"/>
 <title>{embed:page_title} &mdash; The Engine City Times</title>
```

The format of the embed variable is just like a normal variable, except we prepend embed: to the variable name. This differentiates it from normal template variables.

With that set, now when we view a news article on the *Engine City Times* website, the title tag will be populated with both the name of the website (hard-coded into the template) and the title of the article we're viewing (using the embed variable), as shown in Figure 9.5, on the facing page. Here's what the title tag looks like if we viewed the source of the page:

```
<head>
 <meta http-equiv="Content-Type" content="text/html;
  charset=utf-8"/>
 <title>Sample News Article &mdash; The Engine City Times</title>
```

---

4. ExpressionEngine parses template tags in a certain order, and this can impact how your ExpressionEngine tags return data. To learn about more about the parsing order of tags, refer to the ExpressionEngine Wiki page: http://expressionengine.com/wiki/Parse_Order/.

Figure 9.5: DISPLAYING THE ARTICLE TITLE USING AN EMBED VARIABLE

This is only one example of how you can use the embed variable to share data between templates. Explore using embed variables in other ways, and you'll learn how flexible and powerful your templates can be.

9.5   Edit Templates Anywhere

Up until this point we've been editing the ExpressionEngine templates in the browser via the built-in template editor. Although this is a simple way to get started, editing in the browser limits you. Like me, you probably have a favorite text editor that you like to use to write and edit HTML code. By working with ExpressionEngine templates as files, you can easily format your code in the text editor of your choice. You also benefit from an easy to way to back up your templates (just download them from the server). Finally, incorporating version control (like Subversion[5]) into your workflow is simple when your templates are saved as files.

For these reasons, work with your templates as files. The flexibility is more than worth the little effort it takes to set it up.

---

5. For a introduction and overview of Subversion, read http://www.alistapart.com/articles/collaboratewithsubversion/.

Enabling Templates as Files

Saving templates as files is not enabled by default in ExpressionEngine, so we'll need to do a small amount of setup first. We will turn the option on, tell ExpressionEngine where to save the templates as files, and, finally, go through each template and save it so ExpressionEngine creates the file.

On the Control Panel home page, click the Design button, and then click Template Manager under Templates. Click the gray Global Template Preferences button at the top of the page.

Here we alter two settings to enable the ability to save templates as files. First, toggle the preference Allow Templates to be Saved as Files? to Yes. Next, we tell ExpressionEngine where to save the templates.

We can save the templates to wherever we fancy, in any location on our server that ExpressionEngine can access. ExpressionEngine comes with a templates directory inside the system/expressionengine directory, which is a convenient place to put the templates. I use this directory to save templates for all of my projects, so let's use that directory for the *Engine City Times* template files, too.

Now that we know where we want to save our templates as files, we need to let ExpressionEngine know.

The last field on the Global Template Preferences page is Basepath to Template File Directory. Enter the full, absolute path to the location of the template directory. The absolute path will differ across web servers, so if you have trouble finding yours, you may want to ask your system administrator or contact your web host.

With the path to the template directory set, click Update to save the changes. Now ExpressionEngine knows where to save the templates, so we just have to go through and save them all as files.

Saving the Templates as Files

Even though we've enabled saving templates as files, ExpressionEngine doesn't automatically save all of your templates as files. You have to do this manually for each template in the system.

Head back into the Control Panel, and go to the site template group. Select the index template. At the bottom of the page you should now see a Save Template as File checkbox. Select the box, and then click Update. ExpressionEngine saves your template to a file, and from now

> ### When ExpressionEngine Can't Find the Template File
>
> A common error when moving a website to a new server or host is that the template path is incorrect. When this happens, ExpressionEngine will fall back to the last version of the templates saved to the database. Because you have been editing your templates as files, the templates in the database are most likely out-of-date. If you move a site and see that the pages don't have your most recent changes, the culprit is most likely an incorrect path to the templates directory.

on it will read from the template file instead of from the database when using the template to display content on the website.

You can now log in to your server via FTP (or look in your file system, if you're developing locally) and see the template inside the templates and site directories. ExpressionEngine will automatically create directories for each of your template groups when the first template from that group is saved as a file.

Since ExpressionEngine is pulling your template code from the file (as opposed to from the database), any changes you make to the file will be rendered in the browser. If you decide you want to edit a template from within the ExpressionEngine Control Panel, you can still do that; ExpressionEngine will pull in the template from the static file and display it for editing. Any changes you make and save will be saved back to the template file only, not into the database.

With ExpressionEngine templates now saved as files, we are free to edit them in any text editor we choose. The increased flexibility will make creating websites with ExpressionEngine easier.

9.6   What We Learned

This chapter demonstrated how to use the more advanced Expression-Engine templating features. With just a handful of tools, we now have the ability to share data between templates, empower users to choose how they want to see the content, and, finally, submit our own content directly to the site. Up next we'll learn how to keep our site running smoothly using optimization.

Chapter 10

Optimizing Our ExpressionEngine Site

With our *Engine City Times* site complete, we now turn our attention to making sure it is responsive and reliable when the throngs of visitors come to read the news.

The performance bottleneck for most database-driven websites is the database. Querying and reading a data set from a database takes longer than if the web server just had to serve up static files (like .html files). Because of this, we need to make sure we take some steps to optimize our ExpressionEngine website so the database doesn't have the chance to become too much of a bottleneck under heavy or even moderate traffic.

The most basic way to optimize an ExpressionEngine website is by using best practices when coding the templates. If you've been following along up to this point in the book, then you know what those best practices are because you've been using them. But sometimes just following good coding practices isn't enough to guarantee that your site will perform when under medium to heavy traffic.

10.1 Setting Permissions and Establishing a Baseline

Before we get started, we need to make sure ExpressionEngine is able to create and save the cache files. All cache files created by ExpressionEngine live in the cache directory, which is located in your system directory. This is something we did earlier in the book, but it's worth checking again to make sure the cache directory is Writeable on Windows and set to Read & Write or 777 on Unix or Mac OS X. If you're not seeing the cache files created after implementing one of the caching methods that follow, you should double-check that your cache directory has the proper permissions.

We also want to measure how effective these optimizations are for the *Engine City Times* website. To do this, we'll enable some debugging output, so we can see how many queries it takes to render the home page without any caching enabled at all. After implementing each caching method in this chapter, we'll once again look at the number of queries and compare them to the baseline query count.

To enable the debugging output, we use the Admin button in the Control Panel and choose System Administration and then Output and Debugging Preferences. Toggle the Display Output Profiler option to Yes. Click Submit to save the changes. If you're logged in as Super Admin, ExpressionEngine will now show all of the queries used to render the website pages as well as some benchmarks and other application information as shown in Figure 10.1, on the next page.

Reload the *Engine City Times* home page, and scroll down to the bottom. One of the gray boxes you see contains every query needed to render the page. Right at the top of the box is the total query count. My count is showing 58 queries to render the *Engine City Times* home page. We'll put this number aside and use it compare against the query count after implementing each of our caching methods.

10.2 Optimizing with Four Types of Caching

Optimizing your ExpressionEngine website using caching will improve site performance and decrease the load on your server so that your site will load quickly for your visitors. We've all visited sites that are painfully slow, but with some caching and optimization we can avoid that.

There are four ways to optimize your ExpressionEngine website using caching. We'll go over each caching method in detail, but here is a brief overview:

- *SQL query caching*: Most of your database query results are saved in a text file and used the next time the server needs to retrieve the same data.

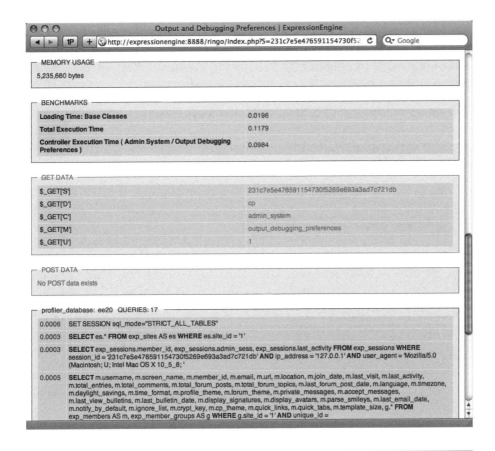

Figure 10.1: Viewing the debugging output

- *Dynamic channel query caching*: This picks up where query caching leaves off, by caching queries that change on every page load.

- *Template caching*: This allows you to cache individual templates by saving an almost-static version of that template.

- *Tag caching*: This gives you finer control over what in your template gets cached and what doesn't. This type of caching is not compatible with template caching.

Enabling SQL Query Caching

In a nutshell, SQL query caching takes all of the output from the queries that ExpressionEngine makes to the database and saves them in a plain-text cache file. Instead of querying the database again, ExpressionEngine can read those cache files when needing the same data. This is a good thing because it is typically faster for the server to read the data from a file than it is to query the database.

SQL query caching is a sitewide setting that will offer you a minimal blanket of optimization. According to the ExpressionEngine documentation, it will reduce by 30 to 90 percent the number of queries needed to run the site.[1]

To enable query caching, log in to the Control Panel, and choose the Admin button at the top. Then choose System Administration, and click Database Settings.

Enable SQL Query Caching should be the third preference. Toggle the radio button to Yes, and save it by clicking Submit. Now all possible queries will be cached, and you should see a reduction in the number of queries needed to render the page.

Let's make sure that the SQL query caching is working as expected. Load the home page of the *Engine City Times* in your browser, and then check the cache directory to see whether ExpressionEngine created a db_cache directory in it. Inside the db_cache directory there should be some more directories and files. If you see this, then SQL query caching is properly enabled and working.

Now let's compare the number of queries it takes to render the home page with the baseline we established at the beginning of the chapter. Scroll down to see the total count of queries. Did the number go down? If it didn't but you see the new cache files in your cache directory, then it is possible that the *Engine City Times* home page doesn't gain any optimization from SQL query caching.

Enabling Dynamic Channel Query Caching

Sometimes the normal SQL query caching cannot cache the more dynamic queries that are produced by the Channel Entries tag pair. This is because the parameters for the Channel Entries tag pair change on every page load (for example when ExpressionEngine uses the current date and time to determine whether to display entries). This extra layer of caching, however, will not work if you use future entries, expiring entries, or random entries. Enabling dynamic channel query caching

---

1. http://expressionengine.com/docs/general/caching.html#query_caching

using any of those three types of entries will give unpredictable and incorrect results.

We're not using any of the three types of entries for The *Engine City Times*, so we're going to go ahead and enable dynamic channel query caching.

In the Control Panel, select the Admin button, and then under Channel Administration select Global Preferences. Look for the Cache Dynamic Channel Queries preference and toggle it to Yes. Click Submit to save your changes.

Let's go back to our browser and reload the *Engine City Times* home page. ExpressionEngine should have created a sql_cache directory and inside it should be some cache files.

Now check the query count at the bottom of the page; it should be less than the baseline we established earlier. You should have saved around seven queries by enabling dynamic channel query caching.

Dynamic channel query caching and SQL query caching are both systemwide settings. The next group of optimization settings give your finer control of how and where you optimize your ExpressionEngine website.

Template Caching

Template caching allows you to have ExpressionEngine cache individual templates; you specify which templates you want to cache and which you don't (by default no templates are cached). When ExpressionEngine caches a template, it saves an almost-static version of that rendered template to a file and uses it to display the page to site visitors until the cache expires and is reset. The reset of template caches are time-based and triggered by certain actions, such as adding a new entry or comment.

Template caching is enabled on a per-template basis, so we need to specifically tell ExpressionEngine to cache the templates. To do this, we go into the Control Panel and choose the Design button, click Templates, and then click Template Manager. We will enable caching on the home page template, so select the site template group and then click Edit Preferences to the right of the index template (see Figure 10.2, on the following page). Find the preference called Enable Caching, and toggle it to Yes. In the next column, set the Refresh Interval value to 60. This tells ExpressionEngine to delete the old cache file and create a new one every 60 minutes.

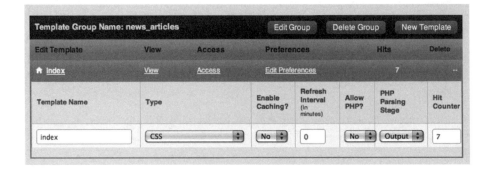

Figure 10.2: TURNING ON TEMPLATE CACHING

The preference will be automatically updated, and now ExpressionEngine knows to cache the site home page template.

Caching Embedded Templates

When we built out the *Engine City Times* templates, we created embedded templates of commonly used template parts (see above, Section 5.3, *Embedding Reusable Code*, on page 80) so we didn't repeat the same code in different templates. These embedded templates are not automatically cached by their parent templates (the template in which they are embedded), but instead caching must be enabled just like with any other template.

For the *Engine City Times* website, the embedded templates are in the includes template group. Just like we did with the site index template, we select the includes template group. For the templates we want to cache, we choose Edit Preferences and toggle Enable Caching Yes. Go ahead and enable caching for all of the templates in the includes template group.

Checking for Results

Load the *Engine City Times* home page in your web browser, and then navigate to the cache directory (inside your system directory); you should see a directory called page_cache. Inside that directory will be the cache directories and files for any templates you set to be cached. Now when you load the *Engine City Times* home page, ExpressionEngine will use the cache file to display the page instead of completely building it dynamically.

> ### Template Caching Trumps Tag Caching
>
> In the game of caching, template caching will always override any tag caching set in the same template. So, if you set ExpressionEngine to cache your index template *and* enable tag caching on one or more tags, the entire template will be cached, and the individual tag cache parameters will be ignored.

With our templates cached, check the number of database queries needed to display the page.

Tag Caching

Tag caching gives us the finest control of all the caching methods described in this chapter. Unlike template caching, which caches the entire template, tag caching allows us to selectively cache certain tags inside a template. This can be useful if you have one tag pair in a template that outputs data that rarely changes while the rest of the template is more dynamic.

Just like with disabling unneeded queries, there is no systemwide preference to enable tag caching. We just place the cache parameter in the tag we want to cache, and ExpressionEngine does the right thing.

In the *Engine City Times* website, a good candidate for tag caching is the category list that lives in the sidebar. The list rarely changes, so there's no reason to query the database for every page load, but other parts of the template may need to be cached less aggressively. That's the real value tag caching; we can cache different parts of a template based on actual need instead of applying one blanket caching setting to the entire template.

As you recall from Chapter 5, *Making the Pages*, on page 67, the category list lives inside an embed template called sidebar in the includes template group. Let's open that template and implement tag caching on the list of categories.

> ## Joe Asks...
> ### Can I Use Tag Caching on Any Tag?
>
> Yes. Tag caching will work on any ExpressionEngine tag in your template. It doesn't matter if this tag is for a third-party add-on or one that is native to ExpressionEngine; the output of the tag will be cached.

Go to the tag pair that populates the list of categories. It should look like this:

`OptimizingYourSitesPerformance/tag_caching.php`

```
{exp:channel:categories channel="news_articles" style="nested"
id="category-nav"}
 <a href="{path="news_articles/page"}">{category_name}</a>
{/exp:channel:categories}
```

To tell ExpressionEngine to cache the output of this tag, we add two more parameters to the categories tag: cache and refresh. The cache parameter with a value of yes tells ExpressionEngine to cache the output of the tag, and the refresh parameter tells ExpressionEngine how often (in minutes) to recache the output. Since the categories will rarely change, we're going to give the refresh parameter a value of 720, which means this cache will reset every twelve hours.

With the category list cached, reload the *Engine City Times* home page. The list should be cached by ExpressionEngine, and a new tag_cache directory should appear in your cache directory. If it does, you know that tag caching is now properly implement for the category list. Don't forget to check the number of queries required to render the page.

10.3 Disabling Unneeded Queries

You'll recognize this method of optimization because we learned about it in Chapter 5, *Making the Pages*, on page 67. As we were building the *Engine City Times* website, we used the disable parameter in the Channel Entries tag pair. You might not have been aware of it then, but you were already optimizing ExpressionEngine!

OptimizingYourSitesPerformance/disabling_queries.php

```
{exp:channel:entries channel="site" disable="pagination"
 limit="5"}
```

The disable parameter tells ExpressionEngine to not bother querying the database for specified data. In the previous code example, we're telling ExpressionEngine to perform the queries needed to set up pagination of the entries it retrieves. We're not going to use pagination, so there's no need to query for the data. Multiple data types should be separated by a pipe (|). This is a very precise optimization method and one that you should get into the habit of implementing as you build your website.

You can disable five different types of data from within the Channel Entries tag:

- categories
- category_fields
- custom_fields (disables all custom field data)
- member_data (disables all member data, like entry author name)
- pagination

If we wanted to disable all six, the tag would look like this:

OptimizingYourSitesPerformance/disabling_queries.php

```
{exp:channel:entries channel="site"
disable="categories|category_fields|custom_fields|
member_data|pagination" limit="5"}
```

There is no global preference to enable or disable this optimization feature. Simply add the parameter to any Channel Entries tags, and ExpressionEngine will not fetch the unneeded data from the database.

10.4 Optimizing for High Traffic

Many high-traffic websites are built on ExpressionEngine. One of the most popular was the Change.gov site put up in 2008 by the Obama Administration transition team. This site received such massive amounts of traffic that they worked closely with EllisLab, the developers of ExpressionEngine, to add some functionality to ExpressionEngine for high-traffic situations.

Tracking Preferences

The functionality added for the Change.gov website is called *tracking preferences*. These settings allow you to control how and if Expression-

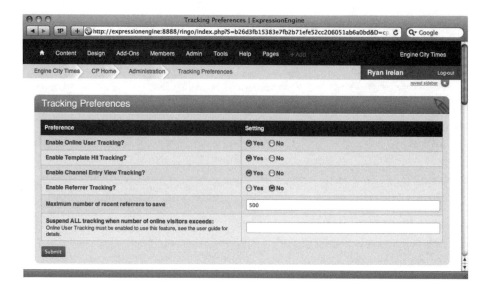

Figure 10.3: DISABLING TRACKING PREFERENCES FOR IMPROVED SITE
PERFORMANCE

Engine tracks template hits, online users, referrer logging, and more.
Some of these tracking features (for example Online Users) require an
update to the database on *every* page load, and under high traffic this
can cause a significant load on the database because it tries to lock the
database table for each update (a requirement of UPDATEs when using
the MyISAM storage engine).

For a lot of websites, this tracking isn't required and can be reduced
or turned off completely by using the tracking preferences. These are a
handful of user-defined options that can reduce the amount of tracking ExpressionEngine does on every page load, thereby reducing the
number of database UPDATEs required.

To access the tracking preferences, go the Control Panel, and click the
Admin button at the top of the page. Click Security and Privacy and
then Tracking Preferences. You should see a form like in Figure 10.3.

- *Enable Online User Tracking*: Turns on and off ExpressionEngine's
  tracking of online users. This is needed if you want to display
  statistics such as "716 Users Online" but is not required for the

majority of ExpressionEngine's functionality. I disable this for almost every single website I build with ExpressionEngine.

- *Enable Template Hit Tracking*: Toggles the hit counting for individual templates. Enable this if you're interested in knowing how many hits a certain template is getting. My suggestion is to turn it off and use a website statistics package (such as the free Google Analytics) for hit tracking. Packages like Google Analytics are more robust and will cause less trouble for your site under heavy traffic.

- *Enable Channel Entry View Tracking*: Enables the hit counting for each channel entry. If you're using ExpressionEngine to measure traffic to your website, then you will want to leave this on. As with Template Hit Tracking, my suggestion is to disable this option and use a full-fledged website statistics package such as Google Analytics.[2]

- *Enable Referrer Tracking*: Allows you to enable the tracking of sites that refer visitors to your website. This can be a useful feature if you have no other statistics package.

Sometimes you don't realize you need to disable these settings until you're already being hammered by a lot of visitors. This could prevent you from logging into your ExpressionEngine Control Panel and updating the settings in the previous list. For situations like these, you can also set these preferences in your config.php file:

- *Enable Online User Tracking*: $config['enable_online_user_tracking'] = '[yes|no]';

- *Enable Template Hit Tracking*: $config['enable_hit_tracking'] = '[yes|no]';

- *Enable Channel Entry View Tracking*: $config['enable_entry_view_tracking'] = '[yes|no]';

- *Enable Referrer Tracking*: $config['log_referrers'] = '[yes|no]';

10.5 What We Learned

In this chapter, we learned the techniques available to tune our ExpressionEngine website for optimal performance. Depending on your website traffic, you may need to implement everything covered or only some

---

2. http://google.com/analytics

Appropriate Hosting and Hardware

Although hosting configuration and hosting hardware are beyond the scope of this book, I want to recommend that you find the appropriate hosting and server hardware for your website. For small, low-traffic sites, this could be an inexpensive shared hosting account. For medium-sized sites, this might be a dedicated server with enough RAM and tuning to handle a significant amount of traffic. For high-traffic websites, this will most likely be a load-balanced setup with multiple servers and expert configuration.

If you use the optimization techniques described in this chapter plus host on the appropriate hardware and configuration, you should have an easier time of keeping your ExpressionEngine site running smoothly.

of the options. As a baseline, I recommend that you at least cache your templates, tags, and queries whenever possible. Even on low-traffic websites this caching will improve the performance and speed of the website for your visitors.

I've included more resources on optimizing your ExpressionEngine website for further reading, and I encourage you to go through all of them and put together your own ExpressionEngine optimization plan of attack.

Resources for Optimizing Your ExpressionEngine Website. . .
. . . http://eeinsider.com/articles/resources-for-optimizing-your-ee-website/
This is a list of resources where you can read more about optimizing your ExpressionEngine website.

10 Largest Websites Running ExpressionEngine. . .
. . . http://www.hopstudios.com/blog/the_10_largest_expressionengine_sites/
Hop Studios has published a short report on ten of the largest known ExpressionEngine websites.

Handling Extreme Traffic with ExpressionEngine. . .
. . . http://expressionengine.com/docs/general/handling_extreme_traffic.html
This is the official documentation page on the preferences available in ExpressionEngine for managing high-traffic websites.

Chapter 11

Extending ExpressionEngine with Add-Ons

It's a common scenario. You're building a website with ExpressionEngine, and your clients want a certain piece of functionality. But ExpressionEngine doesn't have what you want. What do you do? Abandon ExpressionEngine and move to a different CMS? Of course not. This is where add-ons come into play. They extend and enhance ExpressionEngine with functionality that didn't previously exist.

One of the great things about ExpressionEngine is that it doesn't try to do everything. For the most part, it's a lean CMS that relies heavily on outside developers to add functionality based on need.

This chapter will cover the different types of add-ons available in ExpressionEngine and how they fit into the add-on ecosystem. It will also show the best places to find add-ons when you're in need.

At the time of publication of this book, the availability of ExpressionEngine 2–compatible add-ons was very limited. As developers continue to convert their add-ons to ExpressionEngine 2, the pool of available add-ons will increase.[1]

11.1 Exploring the Different Types of Add-Ons

Not every add-on is made equally. ExpressionEngine 2 has four different types of add-ons: plug-ins, extensions, modules, and accessories.

---

1. To keep up-to-date on ExpressionEngine 2 add-ons, visit the EE 2.0 Ready Add-Ons page at http://devot-ee.com/add-ons/ee2.

Each of these add-ons gives us a different amount of control over how and where we extend ExpressionEngine.

Plug-ins, for example, only affect the templates by displaying or altering content. Plug-ins don't have any effect on the Control Panel functionality; that's the domain of extensions. Modules, on the other hand, allow you to create a full-scale application that plugs into ExpressionEngine with template tags and a Control Panel interface.

To get an idea of what each does, let's walk through them, learn about how they work, see how to install them, and view some examples.

Plug-Ins

Plug-ins are the simplest of add-ons. They can be used only in templates and typically affect the output when the template is loaded and parsed by ExpressionEngine. Plug-ins are also the easiest and most accessible add-ons for new developers; a simple plug-in does not take long to create.

Installing Plug-Ins

Before you can use a plug-in, it has to be installed. But don't worry, because it's simple! Only a few steps are involved.

The first step is to find and download the plug-in you want to use. A plug-in typically comes in a .zip file, which contains a folder named after the plug-in. Inside the folder is the plug-in file. All plug-in files will have the same naming convention: pi followed by the name of the plug-in followed by the .php extension.

To install the plug-in, move the entire folder to the third_party directory, which is located in system/expressionengine. You'll notice that there is also a plugins folder inside expressionengine. This is reserved for plug-ins that ship with ExpressionEngine. Any plug-ins you download and install should be placed in the third_party folder. This makes it much easier to back up and manage all of your add-ons since they're all in one folder.

With the plug-in in place, navigate to the Plugins page in the Control Panel (see Figure 11.1, on the next page). Click the Add-Ons button in the main navigation, and then select Plugins. You should see the newly installed plug-in listed in the table of plug-ins. A couple of plug-ins come preinstalled with ExpressionEngine (XML Encode and Magpie RSS Parser), and those should also appear in the list.

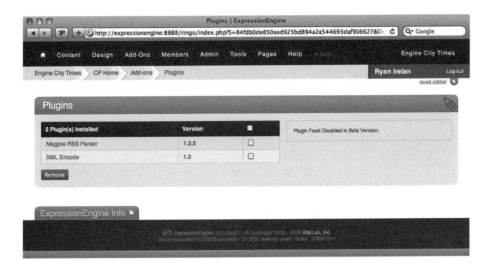

Figure 11.1: Viewing installed plug-ins in the Control Panel

There are no further steps to install plug-ins. Take a few minutes, and find one or two useful plug-ins that interest you. Download, install, and experiment!

Plug-ins You Should Know

The following is a list of plug-ins that are very useful and popular in the ExpressionEngine community. These plug-ins will work on ExpressionEngine 2. Although the list is small now,[2] the number of plug-ins available for ExpressionEngine 2 will grow over time.

- *Allow EE Code*: Put ExpressionEngine template code right in your entry, and ExpressionEngine will parse it. This is very handy for those times when you need dynamic content in an entry field.
- *Low Replace*: Easily find and replace text in your template.
- *EE Gravatar*: A simple way to include gravatars ("globally recognizable avatars") on a site. I use this in the comments section of my website.
- *ClassEE Body*: Dynamically assign a class to the body of your template.

---

2. For a longer list of popular plug-ins and their ExpressionEngine 2 status, visit http://devot-ee.com/add-ons/ee2/faves-plugin/.

\\/ Joe Asks...

Can I Use ExpressionEngine 1.6 Add-ons in Expression-Engine 2?

The release of ExpressionEngine 2 required that all existing add-ons be converted to work on the new and improved ExpressionEngine 2 platform. Therefore, only ExpressionEngine add-ons that have been converted (or created new) will work with 2. The transition from ExpressionEngine 1.6 to 2 will take time, so not every add-on will be immediately available with ExpressionEngine 2 compatibility.

When researching add-ons for your ExpressionEngine 2–powered website, be sure to check whether they have been converted. If not, contact the developer and kindly ask whether there are any plans to convert the add-ons to ExpressionEngine 2.

- *YearList*: Generate a list of years in which there are entries. This is a great way to start building a yearly archive of content.
- *Word Limiter*: Limit text to a specified number of words. This is great for automatically creating excerpts from a long content entry.

Extensions

Extensions allow you to hook into the ExpressionEngine system and add functionality. Unlike plug-ins, extensions do not have any template tags. Developers create extensions by using "hooks" that are made available by ExpressionEngine where they can insert their code to create new functionality.

One example use of an extension would be to do something extra when a user logs in. For example, you may want to make sure that every user sees a list of rules and regulations the first time they log in. An extension could be used to "hook" into the login process and display the rules and regulations to the user, after which they'll proceed to the normal logged-in page.

Installing Extensions

Like installing plug-ins, installing extensions is easy but does require one extra step.

First we need to find and download the extension that we want to use. For this we'll use the First Timer extension I created. This extension allows us to redirect users, upon their first login, to any page on our site (see the earlier example of displaying rules and regulations).

You can download the extension from my website.[3] Unzip the downloaded file, and you should have a folder called first_timer. Inside the folder is the extension file, named ext.first_timer.php, and a language folder. Just like we did with the plug-in, move the entire folder to the system/expressionengine/third_party directory.

You'll recall that with plug-ins we had a one-step installation. Extensions, however, require that we enable them from the Control Panel. Navigate to the Extensions page in the Control Panel (see Figure 11.2, on the following page) using the Add-Ons button and selecting Extensions from the menu. To the right, you'll see a gray Enable Extensions button. In ExpressionEngine, the ability to use extensions is not enabled by default. So, we need to first tell ExpressionEngine to let us use extensions. Click Enable Extensions? to do this. When prompted, click Submit to confirm that you want to take this action. Now extensions are enabled for our site. You only have to enable extensions once to be able to use them. You do, however, have to enable each and every extension you install.

You should see the First Timer extension listed in the table on the page. If it is not, double-check that you moved the first_timer directory to the third_party folder.

The final step in installing an extension is to enable it. We do this by clicking the red "Enable?" text in the far right column of the extensions table (labeled "Status"). By enabling the extension, we tell ExpressionEngine to start allowing it to insert its functionality.

You will also notice two other options listed in the extensions table: Settings and Documentation. The Documentation link will take you to another website (specified by the developer of the extension) that contains information about how to use the extension. The Settings link isn't available for every extension. If it is, you can use it to access the settings for the extension. For the First Timer extension, this includes two settings: the URL to redirect to on first login and the URL to redirect to on subsequent logins.

And now the extension is installed and enabled!

---

3.   http://eequickstartguide.com/downloads/first_timer.zip

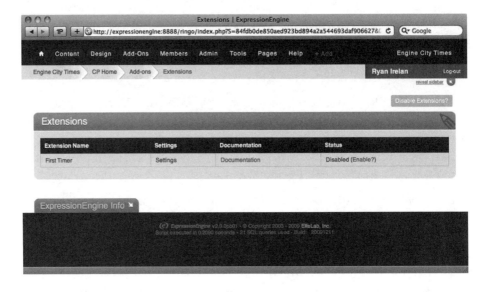

Figure 11.2: Viewing extensions in the Control Panel

On Your Own

With the First Timer extension successfully installed and enabled, take a moment to adjust the settings and try it. Fill in the fields for the URL that should be used for the first login and the URL that should be used for subsequent logins.

Create a new user, and log in to test the functionality of the extension. You may want to also disable the extension to see ExpressionEngine return to its normal login process.

Extensions You Should Know

Here are a few must-have extensions:

- *Low Seg2Cat*: This extension loops through the segments of a URL and matches them to categories. This allows you to create hierarchical category URLs rather than the standard ExpressionEngine category URLs.

- *First Timer*: You can redirect members to a different page the first time they log into your website.

Modules

The next type of add-ons are modules. Modules are more complex than plug-ins and can generally contain more functionality than extensions.

The best way to think about modules are as entire applications that can easily plug into your ExpressionEngine-powered website. Modules can have their own Control Panel interface (accessible through the Modules section) and typically have their own template tags (just like plug-ins).

Most of ExpressionEngine's core functionality consists of a series of modules. Let's take a look.

Navigate to the Modules page of the Control Panel using the Add-Ons button. You should see a long list of modules. All of these put together are what makes up ExpressionEngine. Here are a few examples of modules that are critical to ExpressionEngine:

- *Channel module*: This is what allows you to create and store content in channels. Without this module, you couldn't manage content with ExpressionEngine.

- *Comment module*: This enables the functionality of commenting on channel entries.

- *Member module*: The Member module gives you the ability to have users create and manage member accounts on your website.

All of the modules needed to make ExpressionEngine run are included with the software, but you can also install third-party modules to extend the functionality of ExpressionEngine.

Installing Modules

Similar to installing extensions, modules require that you enable them in the Control Panel before they are available for you to use. I've created a very simple sample module for us to install. The module doesn't do anything per se, but it will allow you to become familiar with how modules are installed.

Download the module,[4] and unzip the file. Just like before with extensions and plug-ins, copy the entire module folder to the third_party folder inside the system folder. Now, we need to install the module from the Control Panel.

---

4. http://eequickstartguide.com/downloads/sample_module.zip

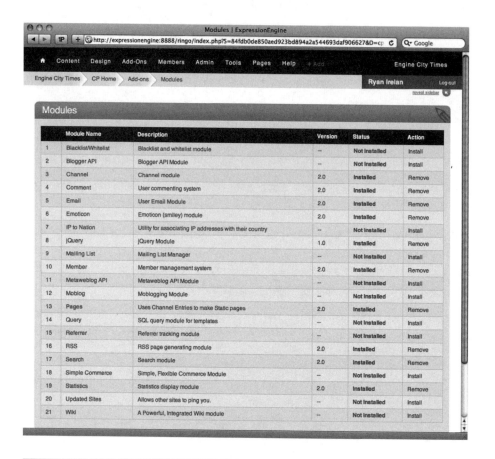

Figure 11.3: VIEWING MODULES IN THE CONTROL PANEL

Navigate to the Modules page of the Control Panel (see Figure 11.3) using the Add-On button in the top navigation. In the table of modules (ordered alphabetically), find Sample Module. Listed should be the module name, description, version number, and status. Our sample module should have a status of Not Installed. To install it, click the Install link. You should receive a confirmation message that it has been installed, and the module name should now be red and a link. This link is what gives you access to the module's Control Panel interface. From here you can configure and use the module. Clicking the module name will bring you to the module's Control Panel interface. For our module, this is just a simple single page.

Figure 11.4: VIEWING THE NEWS AND STATS ACCESSORY IN THE CONTROL PANEL

Click the module name to access our sample module. Since this is just for demonstration purposes, there isn't much there; a typical module would have one or more screens of configuration and administration options.

Accessories

Accessories are the newest type of add-on for ExpressionEngine. They were introduced in ExpressionEngine 2 as a way to make information and functionality easily available in the Control Panel. Accessories live in tabs at the bottom of the Control Panel and are easily accessible no matter where you may be.

Accessories can serve many purposes. An accessory could be as simple as a container for instructions on how to manage the website or a list of links to documentation. It could also be more complex with functionality that allows you to interact with data in the database. The only limit is what developers can do with PHP and MySQL.

An accessory that comes with ExpressionEngine is News and Stats, as shown in Figure 11.4. This accessory gives you real-time information about your ExpressionEngine website and a stream of the latest news from the official ExpressionEngine blog.

Accessories are new, so at first there may not that many available. However, over time, as developers find more uses for them, you should see them pop up regularly.

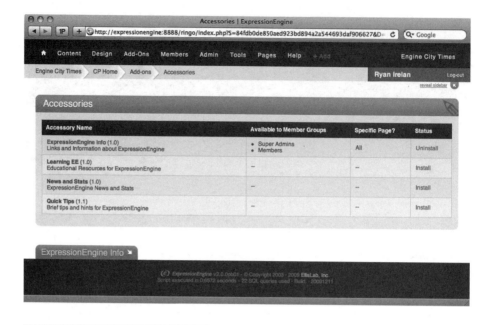

Figure 11.5: VIEWING A LIST OF INSTALLED ACCESSORIES

Installing Accessories

Installing accessories is almost the same as installing the other types of add-ons. Download the accessory you want to install, copy the folder to the third_party folder in your ExpressionEngine install, and then navigate to the Accessories page in the Control Panel, which you can see in Figure 11.5.

There you should see a list of accessories available and their statuses. We want to install the News and Stats accessory. To do so, click the Install link in the far right column. Once the News and Stats accessory is successfully installed, ExpressionEngine will display a success message, and the accessory name will turn red and into a link. Additionally, the status will change to Uninstall. The accessory should now appear as a tab at the bottom of the Control Panel. To view the content of the accessory, click the tab.

Configuring Accessory Preferences

Accessories also give you the ability to determine who can see them (controlled by the member group) and where they appear in the Control Panel. To access the preferences for the News and Stats accessory we

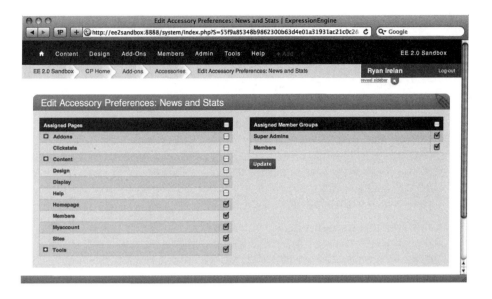

Figure 11.6: EDITING THE PREFERENCES FOR THE NEWS AND STATS
ACCESSORY

just installed, click the accessory name in the table. You should see the
Edit Accessory Preferences page, like in Figure 11.6.

There are two types of preferences we can set for accessories:

- *Assigned Pages*: Here we can select or deselect which pages we
  want the accessory to appear on. This is very handy if your accessory addresses only a certain part of the Control Panel (like the
  Publish screen).

- *Assigned Member Groups*: Restrict access to one or more member groups by selecting the box next to the ones you'd like to see
  the accessory. You may want to show an accessory to the Writers
  member group, for example, of the *Engine City Times* site, but not
  to the Super Admins. Using this preference, you can control that.

Once you have your preferences set, click Update to save your changes.
ExpressionEngine will return you to the Accessories page in the Control
Panel. There you'll see the changes you made reflected in the Specific
Page? column.

> ## Joe Asks...
> ### How Do I Build My Own Add-Ons?
>
> If you have knowledge of PHP and MySQL, you can learn how to build your own add-ons using the official documentation on the ExpressionEngine website: http://expressionengine.com/docs/development/. It walks you through how each type of add-on is built, including some code samples. ExpressionEngine 2 is built on the CodeIgniter PHP framework. Becoming familiar with CodeIgniter will be of great benefit.
>
> Another way to learn how to create add-ons is to download several of them, open them, and look at the code. There is no better way to learn than from someone else's code!

On Your Own

If you'd like to try to install an additional accessory, download[5] the EE Insider accessory, which brings the latest news about Expression-Engine right into the Control Panel. Follow the instructions in Section 11.1, *Installing Accessories*, on page 178 to install the accessory. Good luck!

Now that we've explored the four different types of add-ons, it's important to talk about where they come from and who creates them. Although there are a lot of "first party" add-ons (created by EllisLab), there are even more "third-party" add-ons, created by developers around the world. These developers make up the real power behind Expression-Engine.

11.2 The Add-on Developer Community

One of the lesser known features of ExpressionEngine is the vibrant add-on developer community. There is a large developer base actively creating hundreds of add-ons for ExpressionEngine. Add-ons for almost everything you can imagine have been created, but new ones are still released every single day.

---

5. http://eequickstartguide.com/downloads/eeinsider.zip

Free vs. Paid Add-Ons

As you begin searching for add-ons to use for your Expression-Engine projects, you will undoubtedly notice that some are released for free while others require a paid license (typically per domain).

Many developers release their add-ons for free as a way to give back to the community and help out others who may face a similar problem that their add-on solves. As the user of the add-ons, you should be aware that a free add-on may be more than just free in terms of cost. It may also be free of support, bug fixes, and updates. Typically, paid add-ons have reliable support (through support forums or email), regular updates, and bug fixes.

Both free and paid add-ons, however, are an important part of the add-on developer community.

If a certain piece of functionality is missing from ExpressionEngine, you can be sure that a developer has created an add-on to fill that void. So, where do you find the ExpressionEngine add-ons you need? Well, luckily, there are several resources for you to use.

Add-on Repositories

Because of the nature of how add-ons are distributed (in the forums, on developer websites, and so on), it's not easy to find a comprehensive listing of every add-on that has been created. There are, however, a few places you can use to find almost anything you need when it comes to ExpressionEngine add-ons.

Devot:ee

Devot:ee[6] is an add-on repository created by Ryan Masuga of Masuga Design and curated by both Ryan and the community. Devot:ee has indexed more than 500 ExpressionEngine add-ons and relies on the community to submit new add-ons as they are released. You can easily search for add-ons by type (plug-in, extension, module, or accessory) or by name.

---

6. http://devot-ee.com

In addition to indexing add-ons, Devot:ee also lets users rate, review, and save add-ons as favorites. Devot:ee users can also submit additional information about an add-on to be included in the database.

Devot:ee doesn't store or make available the actual add-on files; you still have to visit the developer websites to download the add-ons you're looking for. Devot:ee just makes it a lot easier to find those add-ons.

When looking for a new add-on, Devot:ee is the first place I go.

Official ExpressionEngine Add-on Library

The Add-on Library[7] at the ExpressionEngine website is much smaller than Devot:ee and not as regularly updated. Add-ons in this repository have to meet certain development guidelines and be approved by EllisLab in order to be included. Despite its small size, it can still be a helpful resource when searching for add-ons for your project.

ExpressionEngine Forums

Although not at all organized like the Official ExpressionEngine Add-on Library or Devot:ee, another place to find add-ons is the official ExpressionEngine Forums.[8] Because of the low barrier of entry, developers will routinely announce new add-ons in the forums and include the add-on file for download. Oftentimes that forum thread becomes the one and only location for information, download, and support of the add-on. With, most likely, hundreds of add-ons in the forums, you can imagine that it becomes difficult to find and keep track of them all.

The ExpressionEngine Forums is typically the last place I look for add-ons because of the low signal-to-noise ratio.

With the help of add-ons, ExpressionEngine becomes even more powerful. Empowered with the knowledge of the different types of add-ons available, how they work, and how to install them, you are now ready to tackle almost any challenging website.

---

7. http://expressionengine.com/downloads/addons
8. http://expressionengine.com/forums

Index

The Pragmatic Bookshelf

Available in paperback and DRM-free eBooks, our titles are here to help you stay on top of your game. The following are in print as of April 2010; be sure to check our website at pragprog.com for newer titles.

Title	Year	ISBN	Pages
Advanced Rails Recipes: 84 New Ways to Build Stunning Rails Apps	2008	9780978739225	464
Agile Coaching	2009	9781934356432	248
Agile Retrospectives: Making Good Teams Great	2006	9780977616640	200
Agile Web Development with Rails, Third Edition	2009	9781934356166	784
Beginning Mac Programming: Develop with Objective-C and Cocoa	2010	9781934356517	300
Behind Closed Doors: Secrets of Great Management	2005	9780976694021	192
Best of Ruby Quiz	2006	9780976694076	304
Core Animation for Mac OS X and the iPhone: Creating Compelling Dynamic User Interfaces	2008	9781934356104	200
Core Data: Apple's API for Persisting Data on Mac OS X	2009	9781934356326	256
Data Crunching: Solve Everyday Problems using Java, Python, and More	2005	9780974514079	208
Debug It! Find, Repair, and Prevent Bugs in Your Code	2009	9781934356289	232
Deploying Rails Applications: A Step-by-Step Guide	2008	9780978739201	280
Design Accessible Web Sites: 36 Keys to Creating Content for All Audiences and Platforms	2007	9781934356029	336
Desktop GIS: Mapping the Planet with Open Source Tools	2008	9781934356067	368
Developing Facebook Platform Applications with Rails	2008	9781934356128	200
Domain-Driven Design Using Naked Objects	2009	9781934356449	375
Enterprise Integration with Ruby	2006	9780976694069	360
Enterprise Recipes with Ruby and Rails	2008	9781934356234	416
Everyday Scripting with Ruby: for Teams, Testers, and You	2007	9780977616619	320
ExpressionEngine 2: A Quick-Start Guide	2010	9781934356524	250
FXRuby: Create Lean and Mean GUIs with Ruby	2008	9781934356074	240
From Java To Ruby: Things Every Manager Should Know	2006	9780976694090	160
GIS for Web Developers: Adding Where to Your Web Applications	2007	9780974514093	275

Continued on next page

Title	Year	ISBN	Pages
Google Maps API, V2: Adding Where to Your Applications	2006	PDF-Only	83
Grails: A Quick-Start Guide	2009	9781934356463	200
Groovy Recipes: Greasing the Wheels of Java	2008	9780978739294	264
Interface Oriented Design	2006	9780976694052	240
Land the Tech Job You Love	2009	9781934356265	280
Language Implementation Patterns: Create Your Own Domain-Specific and General Programming Languages	2009	9781934356456	350
Learn to Program, 2nd Edition	2009	9781934356364	230
Manage It! Your Guide to Modern Pragmatic Project Management	2007	9780978739249	360
Manage Your Project Portfolio: Increase Your Capacity and Finish More Projects	2009	9781934356296	200
Mastering Dojo: JavaScript and Ajax Tools for Great Web Experiences	2008	9781934356111	568
Metaprogramming Ruby: Program Like the Ruby Pros	2010	9781934356470	240
Modular Java: Creating Flexible Applications with OSGi and Spring	2009	9781934356401	260
No Fluff Just Stuff 2006 Anthology	2006	9780977616664	240
No Fluff Just Stuff 2007 Anthology	2007	9780978739287	320
Pomodoro Technique Illustrated: The Easy Way to Do More in Less Time	2009	9781934356500	144
Practical Programming: An Introduction to Computer Science Using Python	2009	9781934356272	350
Practices of an Agile Developer	2006	9780974514086	208
Pragmatic Ajax: A Web 2.0 Primer	2006	9780976694083	296
Pragmatic Project Automation: How to Build, Deploy, and Monitor Java Applications	2004	9780974514031	176
Pragmatic Thinking and Learning: Refactor Your Wetware	2008	9781934356050	288
Pragmatic Unit Testing in C# with NUnit	2007	9780977616671	176
Pragmatic Unit Testing in Java with JUnit	2003	9780974514017	160
Pragmatic Version Control Using Git	2008	9781934356159	200
Pragmatic Version Control using CVS	2003	9780974514000	176
Pragmatic Version Control using Subversion	2006	9780977616657	248
Programming Clojure	2009	9781934356333	304
Programming Cocoa with Ruby: Create Compelling Mac Apps Using RubyCocoa	2009	9781934356197	300
Programming Erlang: Software for a Concurrent World	2007	9781934356005	536
Programming Groovy: Dynamic Productivity for the Java Developer	2008	9781934356098	320

Continued on next page

Title	Year	ISBN	Pages
Programming Ruby: The Pragmatic Programmers' Guide, Second Edition	2004	9780974514055	864
Programming Ruby 1.9: The Pragmatic Programmers' Guide	2009	9781934356081	960
Programming Scala: Tackle Multi-Core Complexity on the Java Virtual Machine	2009	9781934356319	250
Prototype and script.aculo.us: You Never Knew JavaScript Could Do This!	2007	9781934356012	448
Rails Recipes	2006	9780977616602	350
Rails for .NET Developers	2008	9781934356203	300
Rails for Java Developers	2007	9780977616695	336
Rails for PHP Developers	2008	9781934356043	432
Rapid GUI Development with QtRuby	2005	PDF-Only	83
Release It! Design and Deploy Production-Ready Software	2007	9780978739218	368
Scripted GUI Testing with Ruby	2008	9781934356180	192
Ship It! A Practical Guide to Successful Software Projects	2005	9780974514048	224
Stripes ...and Java Web Development Is Fun Again	2008	9781934356210	375
TextMate: Power Editing for the Mac	2007	9780978739232	208
The Definitive ANTLR Reference: Building Domain-Specific Languages	2007	9780978739256	384
The Passionate Programmer: Creating a Remarkable Career in Software Development	2009	9781934356340	200
ThoughtWorks Anthology	2008	9781934356142	240
Ubuntu Kung Fu: Tips, Tricks, Hints, and Hacks	2008	9781934356227	400
Web Design for Developers: A Programmer's Guide to Design Tools and Techniques	2009	9781934356135	300
iPhone SDK Development	2009	9781934356258	576

Better Practices

SQL Antipatterns

If you're programming applications that store data, then chances are you're using SQL, either directly or through a mapping layer. But most of the SQL that gets used is inefficient, hard to maintain, and sometimes just plain wrong. This book shows you all the common mistakes, and then leads you through the best fixes. What's more, it shows you what's *behind* these fixes, so you'll learn a lot about relational databases along the way.

SQL Antipatterns: Avoiding the Pitfalls of Database Programming
Bill Karwin
(300 pages) ISBN: 978-19343565-5-5. $34.95
http://pragprog.com/titles/bksqla

Debug It!

Debug It! will equip you with the tools, techniques, and approaches to help you tackle any bug with confidence. These secrets of professional debugging illuminate every stage of the bug life cycle, from constructing software that makes debugging easy; through bug detection, reproduction, and diagnosis; to rolling out your eventual fix. Learn better debugging whether you're writing Java or assembly language, targeting servers or embedded micro-controllers, or using agile or traditional approaches.

Debug It! Find, Repair, and Prevent Bugs in Your Code
Paul Butcher
(232 pages) ISBN: 978-1-9343562-8-9. $34.95
http://pragprog.com/titles/pbdp

Better Systems

Release It!

Whether it's in Java, .NET, or Ruby on Rails, getting your application ready to ship is only half the battle. Did you design your system to survive a sudden rush of visitors from Digg or Slashdot? Or an influx of real-world customers from 100 different countries? Are you ready for a world filled with flaky networks, tangled databases, and impatient users?

If you're a developer and don't want to be on call at 3 a.m. for the rest of your life, this book will help.

Release It! Design and Deploy Production-Ready Software
Michael T. Nygard
(368 pages) ISBN: 0-9787392-1-3. $34.95
http://pragprog.com/titles/mnee

Ubuntu Kung Fu

Award-winning Linux author Keir Thomas gets down and dirty with Ubuntu to provide over 300 concise tips that enhance productivity, avoid annoyances, and simply get the most from Ubuntu. You'll find many unique tips here that can't be found anywhere else.

You'll also get a crash course in Ubuntu's flavor of system administration. Whether you're new to Linux or an old hand, you'll find tips to make your day easier.

This is the Linux book for the rest of us.

Ubuntu Kung Fu: Tips, Tricks, Hints, and Hacks
Keir Thomas
(400 pages) ISBN: 978-1-9343562-2-7. $34.95
http://pragprog.com/titles/ktuk

Better Methods

Practices of an Agile Developer

Agility is all about using feedback to respond to change. Learn how to • apply the principles of agility throughout the software development process • establish and maintain an agile working environment • deliver what users really want • use personal agile techniques for better coding and debugging • use effective collaborative techniques for better teamwork • move to an agile approach

**Practices of an Agile Developer:
Working in the Real World**
Venkat Subramaniam and Andy Hunt
(189 pages) ISBN: 0-9745140-8-X. $29.95
http://pragprog.com/titles/pad

Ship It!

Page after page of solid advice, all tried and tested in the real world. This book offers a collection of tips that show you what tools a successful team has to use, and how to use them well. You'll get quick, easy-to-follow advice on modern techniques and when they should be applied. **You need this book if:** • you're frustrated at lack of progress on your project. • you want to make yourself and your team more valuable. • you've looked at methodologies such as Extreme Programming (XP) and felt they were too, well, extreme. • you've looked at the Rational Unified Process (RUP) or CMM/I methods and cringed at the learning curve and costs. • **you need to get software out the door without excuses.**

**Ship It! A Practical Guide to Successful Software
Projects**
Jared Richardson and Will Gwaltney
(200 pages) ISBN: 0-9745140-4-7. $29.95
http://pragprog.com/titles/prj

Expand Your Horizons

Web Design for Developers

Web Design for Developers will show you how to make your web-based application look professionally designed. We'll help you learn how to pick the right colors and fonts, avoid costly interface and accessibility mistakes—your application will really come alive.

We'll also walk you through some common Photoshop and CSS techniques and work through a web site redesign, taking a new design from concept all the way to implementation.

Web Design for Developers: A Programmer's Guide to Design Tools and Techniques
Brian P. Hogan
(300 pages) ISBN: 978-19343561-3-5. $42.95
http://pragprog.com/titles/bhgwad

Manage Your Project Portfolio

Too many projects? Want to organize them and evaluate them without getting buried under a mountain of statistics? You'll see how to determine the really important projects (which might not be what you think) as well as the projects you should *never* do. You'll learn how to tie your work to your organization's mission and show your board, your managers, and your staff what you can accomplish and when. You'll get a better view of the work you have, and learn how to make those difficult decisions, ensuring that all your strength is focused where it needs to be.

Manage Your Project Portfolio: Increase Your Capacity and Finish More Projects
Johanna Rothman
(200 pages) ISBN: 978-19343562-9-6. $32.95
http://pragprog.com/titles/jrport

Tune up Your Brain

Pomodoro Technique Illustrated

Do you ever look at the clock and wonder where the day went? You spent all this time at work and didn't come close to getting everything done. Tomorrow, try something new. In *Pomodoro Technique Illustrated*, Staffan Nöteberg shows you how to organize your work to accomplish more in less time. There's no need for expensive software or fancy planners. You can get started with nothing more than a piece of paper, a pencil, and a kitchen timer.

Pomodoro Technique Illustrated: The Easy Way to Do More in Less Time
Staffan Nöteberg
(144 pages) ISBN: 9781934356500. $24.95
http://pragprog.com/titles/snfocus

Pragmatic Thinking and Learning

Software development happens in your head. Not in an editor, IDE, or design tool. In this book by Pragmatic Programmer Andy Hunt, you'll learn how our brains are wired, and how to take advantage of your brain's architecture. You'll master new tricks and tips to learn more, faster, and retain more of what you learn.

• Use the Dreyfus Model of Skill Acquisition to become more expert • Leverage the architecture of the brain to strengthen different thinking modes
• Avoid common "known bugs" in your mind
• Learn more deliberately and more effectively
• Manage knowledge more efficiently

**Pragmatic Thinking and Learning:
Refactor your Wetware**
Andy Hunt
(288 pages) ISBN: 978-1-9343560-5-0. $34.95
http://pragprog.com/titles/ahptl

The Pragmatic Bookshelf

The Pragmatic Bookshelf features books written by developers for developers. The titles continue the well-known Pragmatic Programmer style and continue to garner awards and rave reviews. As development gets more and more difficult, the Pragmatic Programmers will be there with more titles and products to help you stay on top of your game.

Visit Us Online

ExpressionEngine 2's Home Page
http://pragprog.com/titles/riexen
Source code from this book, errata, and other resources. Come give us feedback, too!

Register for Updates
http://pragprog.com/updates
Be notified when updates and new books become available.

Join the Community
http://pragprog.com/community
Read our weblogs, join our online discussions, participate in our mailing list, interact with our wiki, and benefit from the experience of other Pragmatic Programmers.

New and Noteworthy
http://pragprog.com/news
Check out the latest pragmatic developments, new titles and other offerings.

Save on the eBook

Save on the eBook versions of this title. Owning the paper version of this book entitles you to purchase the electronic versions at a terrific discount.

PDFs are great for carrying around on your laptop—they are hyperlinked, have color, and are fully searchable. Most titles are also available for the iPhone and iPod touch, Amazon Kindle, and other popular e-book readers.

Buy now at pragprog.com/coupon.

Contact Us

Online Orders:	www.pragprog.com/catalog
Customer Service:	support@pragprog.com
Non-English Versions:	translations@pragprog.com
Pragmatic Teaching:	academic@pragprog.com
Author Proposals:	proposals@pragprog.com
Contact us:	1-800-699-PROG (+1 919 847 3884)